BOOK REVIEW BY Sist

MW01243661

Congratulations on being a new reader of Patricia Jean Smithyman-Zito's book, *Living in the Now: The Secret to Making Each Day Your Best.*

I found this book to be very helpful in understanding and actually living in the present moment. PJ has combined poetry, storytelling, music and her life experiences into a book that allows the reader to explore their own life's journey while living in the NOW. She is able to help the reader with her probing questions that will enable them to delve deeply into undiscovered places in their life up to this point, and therefore, bring them closer in their relationship with themselves, others and their God. The written book allows the reader space to journal and/or take notes at that moment. Very helpful for concrete changes to really occur!

Our relationship with God is at many levels and this book shows the reader how to discover those levels and to make God alive in their life at each of these levels. I feel blessed to know the author personally and applaud her desire to share her gifts and wisdom with the rest of us. May you be as blessed as I have been by reading this book!

Mary Louise Yurik, RSM

You are smart!
You are handsome!
You are nice!
You are a Steeler Fan!
You are blessed to be
in our family!
Live in the Now! I love you!
Grandma PJ

LIVING IN
THE NOW

LIVING IN THE NOW

The Secret to Making Each Day Your Best

40 Days to Deeper Prayer and Greater Self-Awareness

Patricia Jean Smithyman-Zito

Library of Congress Control Number: 2019906436
ISBN: Hardcover   978-1-7960-3759-3
               Softcover   978-1-7960-3760-9
               eBook   978-1-7960-3758-6

The views expressed in this work are solely those of the author and do not necessarily reflect the views of the publisher, and the publisher hereby disclaims any responsibility for them.

Scripture quotations marked NIV are taken from the Holy Bible, New International Version®. NIV®. Copyright © 1973, 1978, 1984 by International Bible Society. Used by permission of Zondervan. All rights reserved. [Biblica]

Any people depicted in stock imagery provided by Getty Images are models, and such images are being used for illustrative purposes only.
Certain stock imagery © Getty Images.

Print information available on the last page.

For free tips, worksheets, songs and other resources to fully embrace LIVING IN THE NOW, visit LivingInTheNowBook.com/journey

Rev. date: 09/30/2019

To order additional copies of this book, contact:
Xlibris
1-888-795-4274
www.Xlibris.com
Orders@Xlibris.com
550121

Contents

Dedication ix

Acknowledgment x

Introduction ~ Day 1 ~ Awareness of the Little Things.................1

Realizations ~ Day 2 ~ Keeping My Journal of the Little Things ...6

Recognizing Resources ~ Day 3 ~ Fully Engaged in My NOW....10

Become an Expert ~ Day 4 ~ Mulling Over the Meaning.............14

Journal Work ~ Day 5 ~ Exchange Between Planes.....................18

Choosing Choices ~ Day 6 ~ Exciting Change...........................23

Simple Planning ~ Day 7 ~ Habitual Routines...........................28

Mental Plane Pause ~ Day 8 ~ Gateway to More.........................33

Sounding Board ~ Day 9 ~ A Real Journal 37

Crash and Burn Alone ~ Day 10 ~ Crash and Learn with God 42

Eye Opening Experience ~ Day 11 ~ Fully Invested 49

Be Careful What You Wish For ~ Day 12 ~ God Knows Your
Heart's Desire..56

Your Special Journey ~ Day 13 ~ My Special Journey.................62

Risk ~ Day 14 ~ Openness...67

Union ~ Day 15 ~ Radical Change from Test to Yes 72

Walking the Walk ~ Day 16 ~ Talking the Talk...........................76

Perspectives ~ Day 17 ~ Tap My Power......................................81

Never Ending Journey ~ Day 18 ~ Learning to Seek and Find 84

The View ~ Day 19 ~ The Truth..91

Mindfulness ~ Day 20 ~ No More Should or Have To 94

Spiritual Plane Centering ~ Day 21 ~ Deep Work.......................98

Physical Plane Merger ~ Day 22 ~ Meditation.......................... 105

Extend Yourself ~ Day 23 ~ A Reach Through Planes............... 109

Journey of the Soul ~ Day 24 ~ Companions 113

External Work ~ Day 25 ~ Internal Awareness 119

The True Me ~ Day 26 ~ God's Greatest Vision........................ 128

Reach the Pinnacle ~ Day 27 ~ Relationship............................ 137

Wasted Wallowing ~ Day 28 ~ Stuck in the First Two Planes..... 144

Forgiveness ~ Day 29 ~ Immeasurable Love 149

Biggest Influencers ~ Day 30 ~ All Choice 157

Participation ~ Day 31 ~ Unshakable Joy 164

My Destiny ~ Day 32 ~ Spiritual Plane 171

God's Presence ~ Day 33 ~ Spiritual Birth 179

Extend Your Hand ~ Day 34 ~ Tough Love! 186

Being in Love ~ Day 35 ~ Self Worth 190

Become Doubt-Proof ~ Day 36 ~ Know Jesus to Know God 198

Truth Seeker ~ Day 37 ~ Believer 208

I Am the One ~ Day 38 ~ I Plan the Course 217

The Freedom to Choose ~ Day 39 ~ Precious Gifts to Win
or Lose 224

Successful Rituals ~ Day 40 ~ Our End is Just Our Beginning .. 232

Dedication

This book is dedicated to 4 women who have shaped my life and continue to impact my NOW.

Patricia Irene Pigoni-Smithyman, my amazing mother, who at age 93, continues living in the NOW, fully and independently in her own home in sunny Florida.

Nana Anna Capritz-Pigoni, my wonderful grandmother, who lived fully in the NOW until her last few weeks, at the young age of 103!

Venerable Jeanne Chézard de Matel, Foundress of the Sisters of the Incarnate Word Communities, in France, that are now serving around the world.

Mary of Nazareth, mother of Jesus, the Incarnate Word, who shows how a "yes" that is surrendered in the NOW impacts the world.

Acknowledgment

I will never be able to say enough about the gifted, talented and dedicated people who have helped bring my dreams to life: book, workbook, sheet music, e-book, CD music for the book and websites.

I truly want to express my gratitude to all who have helped me take my music to higher levels of professional excellence. Thank you, Sister Rose Miriam, Sister Mary Rose, Barb and Sharon for your tireless assistance and exceptional music skills. I would not have my songs and sheet music to share if not for you amazingly talented women. My deepest gratitude to Bill R. and his musicians for the much needed CD song recording help.

Thank you, dear friend, Mary Fran, for your targeted, generous brainstorming time with me during my final drafting process. Rose, your artistic little sketches compliment my poems and welcome journal work within my book. I tip my hat to my internet guru and online rescuer, Matthew G. for endless support, instruction, web designing and expertise!

I am deeply indebted to my family (Smithymans and Zitos), the Sisters and Associates of the Incarnate Word and my friends, whose amazing journeys have been woven into the fabric of my life, providing course corrections and enabling me to view myself and our world within God's abundant and unconditional love.

Shared, and ultimately understood within the context of our journey's NOW, wisdom pours forth because of our living with and for the other, in Christ Jesus, our Incarnate Word. Also must be noted that thoughts, words and many of my life-changing perspectives here have been influenced by the real-lifetime works of Fr. Richard Rohr, OFM; Dr. Benjamin Hardy, PhD; Oprah Winfrey, Sarah Ban Breathnach and Helen Steiner-Rice.

Lastly, and most importantly, I lift up and applaud my very treasured and amazing Zito family!

Hubby John, our 4 children and their families:
Mark, Maggie, Michael and Mitchell
Lynn, Rich, Brian and Lizzie
Matthew, April and Christian
Lisa and Brandon

I am because of unconditional, incarnational love shared.
PJ Zito

Introduction ~ Day 1 ~ Awareness of the Little Things

It was 1979 when a plane, with 257 people on board, left New Zealand for an exciting sight-seeing tour to Antarctica and back. It is a fact that turbulence and other conditions keep airplanes off their course about 90 percent of their flight time. Traffic controllers, monitors in the cockpit of the plane, pilot and co-pilot focus must constantly make corrections to eventually arrive at each destination. When these corrections are not monitored correctly, we hear of the shocking catastrophe.

The flight coordinates had been off by a mere two degrees for the tour flight out of New Zealand and that put the plane about 28 miles east of where the pilots thought they were. Because of snow blending with the clouds, the pilots didn't know they were in trouble. The incorrect coordinates directed the plane straight into the top of the Mt. Erebus volcano and by the time the instruments sounded a warning the plane exploded on impact killing everyone.

The facts are clear. Small things matter. Every choice has consequences and every consequence changes us. Peace is found trusting in every choice we make. The little things chosen in our everyday lives can cause consequences that are often subtle. Being unaware, they can take us off course. Being aware, they can also help us to remain focused on our sight-seeing journey of life. This story, first written by Dr. Benjamin Hardy, PhD, shapes much of this book's perspective.

What habits and routines have you put in place for piloting your everyday journey here?
Who monitors and helps you control your coordinates to the desired outcomes you've established?
Do you actually have a plan and reason for living your life or are you just reacting to each moment of incorrect coordinates directing you to *somewhere*?

Where are you going with life?
Are you on course? How do you know?

This book is about understanding the sight-seeing tour of your journey here on earth.
It's about being happy in the travel, course corrections and all!
It's about looking at the *process* of monitoring the *progress* at a deeper level.

We are all too busy being busy. We tend to organize and prioritize important and urgent things. We also tend to focus time and energy on a lot of shallow things which consume our NOW moments, like emails, social media sights, playing games and watching TV.

We usually have no idea that we are off of our course until often, we are hitting the wall, exploding on impact to yet another issue we must react to or deal with.

For example, have you ever decided to watch a Facebook video suggestion and look up two hours later? Oh, you have been lost in your NOW!

I want to reduce the noise, the clutter, the hustle of my NOW. I want to be in control of my energy, my thinking, my listening, my praying and my choices to be a human BEing, not a human DOing.

Ready to fly? Can you pause to examine where you've been and where you're headed on your journey? Are you open enough to see what's holding you down? How do we actually examine the plotted course? Are there course corrections necessary for our current NOW?

Correcting the course is not hard or scary. The little things make up the big journey of life.

If this resonates with you, let's start living in the NOW and exploring the journey because the only thing that really holds us down is our mind!

Join me as we find and fuel our moment-by-moment NOW to start leading a truly happy life filled with purpose, passion and personal power!

Chinese Proverb: *"The best time to plant a tree was 20 years ago. The second best time is NOW."*

Are you really happy with your NOW? We are always invited to make the changes that really matter, NOW!

The little things mentioned above are many. Our flight plan for today is to become more aware of all the moments that make up our day. Seize the moment, and a pen, to write your personal observations found within each sentence and question written after Ben Hardy's opening story. Take all the time you need! Trust that your elucidations will surface significant commentary on your present NOW.

I Admire You – Introduction Poem

I wish I knew you better than I do
I would like to let you know that I admire you

I don't suppose you'd be quick to agree
I'm sure you never see what others see

If I could chance to watch you from afar
I'd see evidence of goodness surrounding who you are

A quiet humbleness would probably be
Your attribute of goodness, so impressing me

If I would come and mention this to you
I'm sure you'd look away, not knowing what to do

So that is why I'm writing you this line
I simply want to share these thoughts of mine

Your life enables love and hope to grow
The little things you notice make it so

There is only one task here today. Stop your life on purpose to choose getting back to living fully within each moment, resurrecting your precious NOW within the little things! Start writing and really break down the little details of where you are in your NOW, right NOW!

"A journey of a thousand miles begins with a single step." Lao Tzu

_____

_____

_____

_____

_____

_____

_____

_____

_____

_____

_____

_____

_____

_____

_____

_____

_____

_____

_____

_____

_____

_____

_____

Action Step: (Physical Plane)

Please implement drinking a glass of filtered water upon rising, at mid-morning, at mid-afternoon and about 2 hours before retiring for the night. A little thing your body will love!

I am still learning how to be still before an incomprehensible God. I have loved with all my heart, but not always as a wise, open, emptied individual. When busy about many things, my life would run in fits and starts while I lived what I claimed to be an active-contemplative lifestyle. I write now to explore awareness of the physical, mental, and spiritual planes within which we live. I think I'm learning how I've lived my life backward.

The blessing that has come from my many years of dynamic involvement, though, is what I focus and speak of in my personal journey now. I have touched and have been touched by hundreds and thousands of lives. In all that I have become, I have built an edifice of prayer life around some beautiful people. All are hurting individuals, generous saints, and humbled sinners rolled into one on the journey of life. Bends in the road of life are straight paths in God's love plan for us!

I have learned from my companions on this journey of the realities of life, and as the Word (Jesus) has become flesh for me, I have written. It is a most intense challenge in life that we learn to carry fewer burdens, live fully in each moment, and celebrate who we are in God who loves us unconditionally. So I have attempted to write and sing about the wonders of life and the hurts in life. Through these writings and songs, I heal, grow, and express my prayers of wonder and new awareness within God's unfathomable mercy and grace.

This book is a compilation of my years of journaling. I pray that it will serve as a springboard to spiritual wonderings and spark visions and dreams, drawing you more deeply into your love life with God and with yourself.

People like to talk about being spiritual and not religious. The truth is religion is only meaningful and authentic when there is a "practice" in place. Tools are offered in this journey/process to access the experiences and awareness, rich in insight, healing and spiritual power. As with yoga, voice, dance, musical performance or just walking, additional practice creates what works for you in the expressions of your own person. It is my prayer that you will read this, work within the structured suggestions and plot the flight-plan that is right for your journey.

What are the aspirations of your heart? As I share my journey, I bid you to journey with me as we creatively explore the ponderings and promises that are gifts of God's love. Are my writings really grammatically sound? Are the poems and songs really true to the rules of writing poetry or composing music? Well, probably not! Have I used words or phrases unknowingly from someone else's work? I hope not, and if I have, it was most certainly unintentional, and I ask for forgiveness. I blend experiences of my heart, mind, soul, and probably a little ego into everything, and then that "everything" pours out! I endorse all motivations you muster up to do the same! Want to use my words? No problem. Be my guest!

I am really writing to myself, you know. I always am reminded that God has a hand in all our efforts, and I try to listen, learn, and expand just a bit more. Once you begin your new journey, you will find this to be true for you as well. I highly recommend spending time in the presence of your true self and your faithful God. The rewards are out of this world!

Our journey within this book is to be a slow and in-depth endeavor of discovery and self-actualization. The flow of synchronicity will come in time, with patience and hard work. Our outpouring is to be a disciplined self-engaging time of inward growth and that takes energy. Begin your own journal work by always going back over the section just read to break it apart. Write down the little things of change, or comments made or your own inspiration to make the section apply to you and your changing journey today.

"There is divine beauty in learning. To learn means to accept the postulate that life did not begin at my birth. Others have been here before me, and I walk in their footsteps." Elie Wiesel

_____

_____

_____

_____

_____

_____

_____

_____

Action Step: (Mental Plane)

Creative inspiration and positive motivation can come from outside sources. May I suggest picking up some type of outside inspiration to read in tandem? Choose a book similar to:

The Road Less Traveled by M. Scott Peck
The Happiness Project by Gretchen Rubin
The Year of Magical Thinking by Joan Didion
The Path Made Clear: Discovering Your Life's Direction and Purpose by Oprah Winfrey

More information and resources will be available as we continue our journey so stay in your precious NOW and let's systematically look at the little things without being too distracted.

I am blessed to finally be able to find a way to recognize my life events, both past and present, as coordinates or traffic monitors for so much more meaning, blessing, purpose and wealth in my NOW. I want to share this awareness and show how these events can be a model for your own flight plan or treasure hunt into the collection of occurrences you call your life. The more proficient one becomes at recognizing beauty and value, the easier it is to go through each day aware of a deeper meaning as life unfolds. The unseen energetic connection of these events and activities called a life is no less than God, the ground of all being, the Divine, the Universe, or whatever descriptive label you choose. Establish your terminology to allow your reading and thinking journey here to be comfortable moving forward and inward. I will use various names and/or phrases but always meaning the source of all being, God.

Do you spend time tapping the inner resources you already possess? Do you pray? Do you call your quiet times meditation? Is there a habitual structure supporting your sacred times? What ways or means do you use to express your thoughts, desires, dreams, concerns, and fears? There will always be a lot of questions that you and I probably can't really answer quickly or easily. This is, after all, a lifetime journey, filled with more turbulence and threatening conditions than anyone cares to conquer. So, for all of us, as precious people journeying to God, may this book be a springboard to know yourself and a flight plan that is focused on staying the course each moment. I long to recognize and appreciate the holy abundance of moment-by-moment awareness. Living meaningfully is about thriving and appreciating life rather than merely surviving. This applies to good times, sad times, wise choices and regrettable mistakes!

Writing has been my tool and my salvation. Sharing my work with you is my joy and my way of living meaningfully in the *NOW.*

("NOW" is my tag-term for "awareness of the moment you are actually in, during that moment!")

Treasures ~ Poem 1

I want to become a writer,
Something I've always envisioned I'd do.
I only know I want to try,
So I'm mentioning it to you.

Writing seems to surface my resources,
Something I've always labored to do.
I really feel quite able now
Since mentioning it to you.

My creative sparks keep igniting,
Something I've always been able to do.
But to keep it burning brightly,
I'd like to share this love with you.

Thanks for patience as I pour out my soul,
Something I've always needed to do.
We'll slowly become what we're called to become.
Such treasures are way too few!

This book is evidence of my lifetime of using inspirations as my grounding and my springboard. Writing for a lifetime, journaling, is something from which everyone can benefit. I invite you to journal too! As I have said, this book is really designed to be used as a tool, a springboard, for your own writings and musings and as meditation starters. It is to be more than just a book you would pick up and read from beginning to end. You may feel yourself in exactly the same position as many of the stories, songs, and poems within these writings. I am hoping to pique your interest with something I will say, so you will do your own due diligence on the topic, becoming more aware of the holy abundance a new path can provide for you.

God does not protect us from all the bumps in our journey through life, but God does walk beside us. God asks of us a faith so pure and uncompromising that only purposeful self-discipline, daily prayer, and I believe, a focus on the Incarnate Word, God choosing to live fully as a human person, could enable us to live up to this demand.

The events, comments, sorrows, criticisms, apparent defeats we experience seem to deafen us to the Divine voice desiring to guide us in love. The secret is this: the very things which initially deafened us to hearing and responding to God's voice are the elements of the deeper message God has for us. Recognizing this is what we journal about to better focus on the abundance within our NOW.

"People are like stained-glass windows. They sparkle and shine when the sun is out, but when the darkness sets in their beauty is revealed only if there is a light from within." Elizabeth Kubler-Ross

Now, begin your own journal work today by going back over the section just read and break it apart. Write down the resources resonating for you. Add your personal comments or your own revelations found in this section that apply to you and your changing journey today. Go deeper.

_____

_____

_____

_____

_____

_____

_____

_____

_____

_____

Action Step: (Spiritual Plane)

Stretch and breathe every morning from now on, before you even
get out of bed. Take 2 minutes to deeply breathe in the blessings of
another day of life, for it is indeed a gift. Pray for all who struggle to
be fully in their NOW and send them your energy and your blessing
as you exhale. Ask, in words of conversation, for all you need to stay
in your NOW for this new day ahead. Step out of your bed, aware
of your resources burning brightly as you begin your day. Don't
forget to drink your water and read from your book of motivation or
inspiration. We are forming habits!

By employing the process described in this book, one will experience the joy and full energy awareness of a life lived in surrender. What does that sentence mean? That is what we are trying to do as we journey. Take apart what is before us by asking what does that mean, really?

When is a box more than a box, music more than melodious sound, pizza more than dough and toppings? Start with the box. This six-sided object with a lid and interior space has increased value, to the degree of becoming quite priceless, when combined with certain contents and/or future purpose. A black velvet ring box becomes a future promise of a great commission for the jeweler, hope for a lifetime of love and family to suitor, or a dream both fulfilled and just begun for the recipient. When is a box more than a box? The meaning is in the imagination of the beholder. The perceiver holds the meaning.

How about that pizza? Shelly sees pizza and thinks, "I can't eat it because it has gluten. I am missing out." Sharon remembers eating pizza every Friday night with her family so she thinks, "I love pizza and this is the beginning of the weekend and family fun." Matthew loves to go out for pizza and beer with friends so he thinks, "We all have such a great time when we meet for pizza together!"

Consider this book a way to become an expert in valuing life events, not unlike the Antique Roadshow experts. Week after week, audiences around the world are amazed to find out that the umbrella holder in the doorway is a vase from Ming dynasty, and aren't they glad they kept it when they moved.

Are you an expert when it comes to the physical plane we live in? If you are healthy, strong and pain free because of wise choices over the years, yes. Let's consider becoming a health nut! Over the next 10 days, clear out your cabinets and fridge of the foods you think are "healthy" (or have been deceived by clever food labels into believing are healthy), but in reality, are fat-storing traps in disguise.

Over the next ten days, I want you to eliminate all:

whole grain breads
whole grain cereals
whole grain crackers (more of that wheat that's killing you)
soy milk
tofu or "veggie burgers" (non-fermented soy can be harmful to your hormones - fake estrogen)
orange juice (loaded with too much fructose that raises your triglycerides)
apple juice
skim milk or homogenized milk
margarine (deadly trans fat or even "MegaTrans")
pre-packaged "diet" dinners
sport drinks
protein bars (most are candy bars in disguise!)
overly processed meal replacements (with more junk than healthy ingredients)
rice cakes (massive blood sugar spike)
pasta (more wheat to age you faster)
diet ice cream or diet desserts
so-called "energy" drinks
low-fat foods (usually replaces fat with more sugar)

The first few days will be hard because it will be a basic cleansing, detoxifying, and the eliminating of wheat, dairy and sugar from your diet. You may hate me then. I hope you will dig deeply and eat only pure, natural, fresh food just to see how our physical plane impacts the mental and spiritual planes. This is not a diet. This is not about starvation. This is about changing your body on the inside and giving it a tune-up. God made us to live forever. Our body transforms itself constantly when it has the proper nutrition. You know you have wanted to be healthier. NOW is the time. Honor your temple. Find your deeper inner convictions, NOW!

Write as the days unfold. List what you've stopped putting in your body and listen to how your body is responding. Come to know which foods impact you negatively. Pay attention to change.

Action Step: (Physical Plane)

Be aware of how you will eliminate items from your list. Spend time planning substitutions for what you will not be eating any more. Shop with a prepared list of what foods to buy for cooking your healthier meals. Remember that your goal is to be healthy by cleansing the body of toxins and foods that are "fake" or compromised. Eat every 3 hours. Drink water, coffee or tea only.

This is my prayer: "Oh God, correct our course, open our minds and hearts, cleanse our bodies, heal our wounds as we journey together. Forgive our sins and failures, and bring us into the wonder of Your abundant and omnipotent love. In Your mercy, allow us to live long enough to discover You here and now and love as Jesus loves."

Take heart, child of God! We are all in the same boat! Becoming the master of our fate will push us in ways we could never have imagined! We are focused on the physical plane because that's us! It is also the center to free us enough to wrap our head and heart around the discipline needed to truly change. How are you feeling? Have you jumped into your food list with both feet? Just like getting into a cold swimming pool, the less painful approach is to jump in! Ponder this:

If your doctor told you that you were deathly ill and gave you the negative food list on page 15 as a way to save your life, you would do it. So, do it NOW before you are sick!

The flight plan for our living in the NOW journey will be broken into three categories. Patiently peruse these beginning course corrections to differentiate the 3 planes and understand their broad parameters.

Physical Plane Tips ~ Course Corrections #1

- Saying I will change isn't enough.
- I have to focus on actual healthy choices that will support me and strengthen me in making my life better, physically.
- How do I take care of myself?
- I will write down everything I do and everything I eat and drink for two or three days.
- Then, I will look for critical answers.
- All through the night, my body is fasting, repairing and healing. My body needs two full glasses of water to flush out toxins and eliminate the "bad" it worked on all night. Water will also hydrate my brain and my organs so they can work properly.
- Breakfast should consist of some type of protein since my body has fasted for at least eight hours during sleep.

- Lunch should be my "heavy" meal, with lots of raw foods and a good bit of protein because my body has time to digest during the afternoon hours.
- Dinner should have plenty of cooked vegetables, a small salad and a small portion of protein.
- I want all digestion work completed way before going to sleep. That way, my body can work on replenishing, repairing, and resting, rather than on digesting food all night. I should remember to eat fruits for mid-morning snacks and a few nuts and seeds for an afternoon snack to keep my metabolism working and my cravings at bay.
- Am I drinking eight glasses of purified water every day? Ninety percent of all degenerative diseases begin in the colon and thrive because we are not hydrated enough to flush them out.
- Want more information on health and wellness for your physical plane work? Just visit us at: www.LivingInTheNowBook. com/physical
- I suggest you view the film Eat, Pray, Love; book by Elizabeth Gilbert

Mental Plane Tips ~ Course Corrections #1

- Saying I will change isn't enough.
- I have to focus on changing how I think things through and how I "self talk" throughout my daily activities and encounters.
- Stop and think of decisions made as a younger person for which you are grateful. Thank yourself for moments that pivoted your journey.
- Listen critically to your own mental dialogues to honestly evaluate your attitude.
- I am always stepping off to the side of myself to watch what I am doing and saying as situations unfold.
- Ever watch yourself during a meeting or at lunch? Pretend you are running a movie camera and watch yourself through that lens.

- Write about your observations, and without any criticism or judging, state the facts as they are.

Spiritual Plane Tips ~ Course Corrections #1

- Start your morning with your 2-minute gratitude stretching in bed. Work up to two glasses of water and a five minute "quiet sit" before anything else begins your day.
- If you must, set your alarm for about ten minutes earlier, so that the daily routine isn't too disrupted.
- As you sip and sit, feel refreshed and focused but try not to make it a work session.
- This isn't when you are to plan your day's activity schedule. This is a time to line up your energies, to breathe deeply, to tap your inner core strength-source, to empty your mind of everything and to fill your heart with peace.
- Just five minutes, for now, will fill you. Enjoy!

Taking our thoughts and self-talk up a notch, let's believe what we are going to read next. I would like you to read the next section out loud! Ready?

"I keep a positive view of myself. When I think about the person whom I have become, I am filled with joy. I am proud of who I am. I live by my values and I try to make a difference in the lives of others. *Instead of being my own worst critic, I choose to be my greatest cheerleader.* I encourage myself with positive thoughts because it is the best thing I can do for my self-image."

Nice! Thinking changes everything! Your body believes what your mind tells it.

"Positive thinking is more than just a tagline. It changes the way we behave. And I firmly believe that when I am positive, it not

only makes me better, but it also makes those around me better."
Harvey Mackay

Start your own bookwork right here, right now with whatever thoughts
easily coming to the surface! Targeting your mental plane, think about
all we are putting together here on day 5. This is a big day and your
flight plans are critical to your future course corrections so dig deeper!

_____

_____

_____

_____

_____

_____

_____

_____

_____

_____

_____

_____

_____

_____

_____

_____

_____

_____

_____

_____

_____

_____

Action Step: (Mental Plane)

Wow, that is enough thinking for today! Allow whatever surfaced to be with you until our next encounter begins. Bring the 3 planes to life in your daily routines and speak to others of the positive changes you are experiencing as you purposefully chisel new habits into your NOW.

Ancient wisdom says that muddied waters let stand, clear. Then new images can appear.

Choosing Choices ~ Day 6 ~ Exciting Change

Every moment is really like a new day! Let's begin today's journey with a song in our hearts! Listen to the song! Find the link at the bottom.

December 7, 1969 Words and Music by Patricia Jean Smithyman-Zito.

Audio for all the sheet music you see in this book can be found at

www.LivingInTheNowBook.com/music

I can sing this happy song, truly mean it, and actually believe from the evidence of the world around me that God is my focus of praise and honor. I am excited! Why? I am taking time to stop and see! I am looking at choices for revealing the "real me."

A tree, by its very nature of treeness, does nothing but praise and honor God. Mountains and valleys, oceans, rivers, and seas honor God and proclaim glory just by their creation millions of years ago, their vastness, and their depth or density. That is the physical plane we live in.

We, people of God, however, are given free will as we journey through life on earth. We spend so much of our energy just trying to survive and function in the physical plane and rightly so, but we are also able to make a choice in each moment whether to praise God or not. If only I could get out of my own way to do so. Oftentimes, I see my life flying by without my actually being very involved in the physical, mental, or spiritual planes. How hard does one have to look to capture self-awareness or understand there is a need to even try?

I Choose Change ~ Poem 2

For so many years, my body has been a hawk,
Living on the edge, pushing, diving,
Risking life itself, just to feel alive.
And sometimes, I crumble and cry with regret.

For so many years, my mind has been a caterpillar,
Tightly wrapped in cocoon, dormant, still,
Waiting for the bursting forth of anything.
And sometimes, I anxiously anticipate truly living.

For so many years, my soul has been a dove,
Hiding from the hawk, believing in the butterfly,
Hoping against hope to find refuge.
And sometimes, I eagerly envision life's hope.

For so many years, my heart has been a lion,
Pouncing, roaring, simulating strength and power,
Testing every isolated incident and transparent trend.
Yet sometimes, I freeze with fear of ego's influences.

For so many years, my other self has been a gazelle,
Springing over obstacles, conquering valleys and
mountains,
Alive and believing in the potential hidden within.
And in Mystery's grace, I perceive intrinsic,
intimate Presence.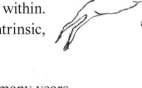

For now, I choose to reflect on so many, many years,
And I will tell you of all I can liken my true self to by
Opening up to risk, trusting, and humbly
believing in love.
And somehow, I choose to be happy becoming *me*.

"The guy who takes a chance, who walks the line between the known and unknown, who is unafraid of failure, will succeed." Gordon Parks

"Life isn't about finding yourself. Life is about creating yourself." George Bernard Shaw

"There are no shortcuts to any place worth going." Beverly Sills

Brene Brown has a TED Talk that over eleven million viewers have watched and it is called "The Power of Vulnerability." She talks about how vulnerability isn't a sign of weakness. Emotional risk is our birthplace of change. Adapting to change is all about being vulnerable and that is all about being fully human and accepting it.

Write of your years past, as if you are an observer, by using *she* or *he* instead of *I* as you journal your thoughts today. Reread the poem "I Choose Change," and use imagery to describe what you are searching for and feeling (ex., my other self is a gazelle).

What areas of your life would you enjoy looking into a little deeper?

What areas of your life do you honestly know you should look into a little deeper?

Judge nothing.

_____

_____

_____

_____

_____

_____

_____

_____

_____

_____

_____

_____

_____

_____

_____

_____

_____

_____

_____

_____

_____

_____

_____

Action Step: (Spiritual Plane)

How about a spiritual vitamin to calm your anxieties going into
events of the day? Repeat this often during your days. Take vitamin
A… "All things work together for good for those who love God, who
are called according to God's purpose." (Romans 8:28)

I Know That I Can ~ Poem 3

Standing in the light, I know that I can be a beacon strong.
Mirroring God's image, I can choose to do no wrong.

Running in life's race, I know that I can be a driven winner.
Often stumbling to the goal, I also know that I'm a sinner.

Walking in deep faith, I know that I can be a believer true.
By living in the NOW, my every step takes me to You.

Resting in God's love, I know that I can be God's precious one.
In savoring such bliss, I find the depths of Incarnation.

Fr. Richard Rohr beautifully expresses "If Jesus is the God-Man, I believe that some radical changes should be taking place in our history, in our faith lives, and in our everyday encounters and relationships. Could it be true that God's Absolute entered into our history? Yes. God's beloved Son was sent to earth. Did we all catch the word *sent*? God, Father, Creator, Authority sent the Son. Jesus didn't say anything about doing this incarnational thing. This was the Father's plan of salvation, long before anything happened in the garden or anywhere else. God absolutely couldn't live without us. The Son was sent because God wanted the "divine family" to be one. This is how we humanly explain an infinitely loving truth. God has chosen us. God desires our yes." Oh, happy day!

What will it take for me to grasp that concept? If only I could stop following the rigid workaholic rules, the expectations of others, the dualistic ego thinking with concerns and desires that control me. Can I be so busy doing so much that I miss the mystical union? I honestly don't want to miss the holy. I want to say my yes and mean it. We are all called to be holy. I can't believe the lie that I'm not good enough.

My course correction is to suspend judging to see others and myself as God sees us.

Have you listened throughout your life to always choose the better life of faith, or can you honestly say you often live by reacting to each next event or circumstance as it presents itself to you? That's what we do as children. When do we make that transition to be totally responsible for our own destiny?

Daily routines can bring needed structure and efficiency to our living. Let's take a look at the benefits of thinking through the things we do automatically, day in, day out. Daily routines can lessen procrastination and anxiety. By establishing daily priorities, we can make decisions about what is most important and what is most beneficial in our NOW. Eliminating times of indecision or planning a schedule to promote healthy habits or working from a prioritized daily, weekly, monthly list streamlines areas of focus and actually frees up time and attentions. The lesser things fade away for those more eminent or more important matters to best receive precious energy. Think about how many habits our morning routines use, for example, which frees our mind for other tasks of the day to be addressed or decided upon. We really do not think about that morning shower or how to brush our teeth, but we certainly did when we were children! We tend to become less tense, more positive, more reflective, and much happier within the familiar building up of structure and planning. Spend time listing your priorities in the little things of one day. Consider establishing a simple plan that can become a habitual routine for the "must do every day" tasks. Becoming proactive is a powerful choice we can apply to small tasks and major responsibilities. Starting small helps me train my brain and my emotions to better use chosen steps and thought-out strategies for dealing with and planning out my moments. It is a challenge to achieve happiness and effectiveness, and it is worth putting time and energy into such planning.

Anxiety, worry, panic, and lack of confidence can be beaten by thinking logically, planning efficiently, and surrendering within prayer. Structures of my time always challenge me. Being a very right-brained individual, I tend to lean toward the dreams and that nebulous yellow brick road going where? So for today, let's grasp on to the concrete, specific, detailed focus of *planning*. Let's expect positive results from the decision to pay attention to structure and eliminate distractions and senseless procrastinations, which often make for a more inefficient and scattered NOW. How do we use the gift of 1,440 minutes each day? It takes 2 five minute timeframes, a total of ten minutes a day, to center and ensure yourself of living more fully in the NOW. Use them or lose them! Go a little deeper to fly higher!

Breathe, relax, and start producing your plan of structured action regarding the little things. Nobody else can live in your precious moments. Oh, how I wish I could get back the ones I've missed!

"You get the best out of others when you give the best of yourself." Harry Firestone

"Behold God beholding you and smiling." Peter G. Van Breemen, SJ

"Contemplative practice might be five or twenty minutes of "dying," of letting go of the small mind in order to experience the big mind, of letting go of the false self in order to experience the True Self, of letting go of the illusion of our separation from God in order to experience our inherent union." Fr. Richard Rohr, OFM

Write out your specific plans for changes in your daily routines. Re-read this day's reflection as you list your ideas. Your list of changes should include decisions made from your journal work for days 1 through 6, too. Lots to remember, huh? Take your list with you to remind you of how you want to structure your time until you actually

move through routines enough to hone new habits for the little things.
Go deeper and hold yourself accountable.

"Your journey begins with a choice to get up, step out and live fully."
Oprah Winfrey

_____

_____

_____

_____

_____

_____

_____

_____

_____

_____

_____

_____

_____

_____

_____

_____

_____

_____

_____

_____

_____

_____

_____

_____

Action Step: (Physical Plane)

Construct your rough draft plans for the little moments, routines and structures for just a very typical day. Let's become more aware of how much time escapes us. Let's lessen some of the chaos and noise on our physical plane with new habits.

"Be still and know that I am God." Psalm 46:11

In the Quiet ~ Poem 4

Early in the morning hours, long before the rising sun,
I place myself in the quiet to ponder all that God has done.
How I need love and grace again, through prayer, to realize
When I place myself in Presence, love just multiplies.

My heart soars efficaciously in the holiness of night,
As I contemplate God's love for me, everything is right.
No words can ever utter what the night's eye can behold
When I make time in the quiet, love's messages unfold.

In the quiet of my inner soul, I hear, I see, I touch,
I place my being in the Word, God loves me so much.
Through prayer and quiet searching, God calls me by my name,
With time and introspection, I am never quite the same.

There's nothing I'll be wanting then in all I'm called to be.
In the quiet, any time or place, God's presence is with me.
Awareness of this blessing, of meeting God in mystery,
Grows deeper every time I pray, and here is where I'm free.

> Praised be the God and Father of our Lord Jesus Christ,
> who has bestowed on us, in Christ, every spiritual
> blessing in the heavens! God chose us in Christ before
> the world began, to be holy and blameless in God's
> sight, to be full of love. God likewise predestined us
> through Christ Jesus to be adopted sons and daughters.
> Such was God's will and pleasure that all might praise
> the glorious favor bestowed on us in His beloved.
> (Ephesians 1:3–6)

In the quiet, I can be still. I am aware of God's presence.

When was the first time you remember your intense connection with someone who was not physically with you? Is there an awareness of not being alone when you are sitting by yourself?

I am connected to you deeply and I am not with you. God is connected to you and is always there, waiting for you to say hello. Your prayer is the movement toward God. That is being with your beloved. "Hello, God!"

Remember what you know as you reread the poem "In the Quiet" slowly and meditatively, applying my thoughts and words to your own prayer.

Being attentive is not a prelude to something else! Being attentive literally puts me in the presence of God.
Where would this awareness make a difference in your daily life?
This is how we can spend some time without structure, agenda, or purpose.
There is a time for structure, and there is a time for no structure.
Ponder.
Realize.

"A new attitude of faith will save me. The favor of God will keep my enemies from defeating me. The creator of the universe holds me in the palm of his hand. The enemy is not in control of my life. Our power is based in God's favor and when I cooperate I am able to tap the fullness of living. My power is based on God's favor. Strongholds are unseen forces and only a humble asking of God's favor will enable me to move forward. God is limited when my faith is limited. I can live a healthy, holy, free, abundant life without negative thoughts by getting up each morning expecting a miracle and believing in God's favor to push me into my destiny." Joel Olsten

Where can evidence of God's plans for me be found?

This journal entry can be done simply, or feel free to add pages if Spirit moves you to write more!

_____

_____

_____

_____

_____

_____

_____

_____

_____

_____

_____

_____

_____

_____

_____

_____

_____

_____

_____

_____

_____

_____

_____

_____

_____

Action Step: (Mental Plane)

Be still, and in your quiet, connect with God.

Sounding Board ~ Day 9 ~ A Real Journal

Let's target today's journey with an internet story.

Rosie and Phil

Rosie is always making things happen. She tells everyone that one of her greatest secrets about completing tasks and making things move in the directions you want is to write things down in a journal. Putting her goals, thoughts, hopes, and dreams on paper helps her actualize what matters the most. It's her secret way to bring her goals and dreams to life, and if you could see how much Rosie happily produces in one day, you would be amazed!

Rosie often reads her journal notes and they always help her to focus her mind on living the life she desires. One of her friends asked her for ideas to help with moving beyond the barriers he had build around his relationships and his own self-thinking. He explained to Rosie that he was not where he thought he would be by the time he hit his 30's, and he was trying to take a good hard look at what structures would help him to change things for the better. Rosie told him to sit tight for a moment as she went into her office. Within a few moments, she returned and handed him a paper listing the journaling strategies she lived by, and lovingly encouraged him to dream every impossible dream and believe in every unbelievable miracle possible! So, he gave her a hug as she gave him her secrets!

Try these journaling strategies to help bring all your self-improvement goals to fruition:

1. Write quickly and passionately. Let the ideas flow onto the paper without dwelling on one thing for too long. Writing in this manner will allow your goals, dreams and wishes to flow out freely beyond what you thought possible! Try setting a time goal and

writing freely without pause until the period ends. Once you're finished, you may be surprised with what you've written and gain new insight and understanding from this activity.

2. Write consistently. You may not be an everyday writer, but formulate a routine to keep your journal flowing. When you write on a daily basis, you'll find a greater consistency to your thoughts and reflections.

3. Set goals and reflect on them. Outline your most important self-improvement goals when you begin your journaling experience. Reflect on them often to determine whether or not you're taking active steps toward achieving them.

4. Try to be honest. You can be completely honest in your journal because no one else will read it but you. Share your secrets, dreams, and desires - even the ones you cannot share with anyone else. Use your journal as a sounding board, and never sacrifice honesty for any reason.

5. Ask yourself tough questions. Self-reflection is an important aspect of self-improvement, and your journal can aid significantly in the reflection process. Ask yourself questions about where you are in life and where you want to be so you can brainstorm the necessary steps in the self-improvement process.

6. Refer back to your past writing regularly. When you have a bad day, look at your positive writing to ease your thoughts. When you feel lost or unsure about yourself, look back over your goals and insights to find guidance. There's a wealth of vital information

in your journal if you use it consistently, and you can turn back to this information to show you where to go next.

At the end of the list that Rosie gave him, Phil saw that Rosie had added a note of her own for him. She surely is a great friend and a wise human being!

Choose a journal that's right for you, Phil. Select a journal that resonates within you, something that you feel comfortable and confident writing in. You can purchase a journal from a bookstore, create your own, or simply collect loose pages in a binder. The right journal will inspire you to use it. Simply putting your thoughts down on paper can help you realize your dreams and focus your attention on what truly matters in your life. Strive to write in your journal as often as you need, and refer back to what you write to help you keep those goals in mind. Journaling is a powerful tool, but is only effective when you're willing to put your passion into it. Be happy and believe in who you are. Life is too short to not live fully in your NOW!
Trust in who you are,
Rosie

"Discipline yourself to do the things you need to do when you need to do them, and the day will come when you will be able to do the things you want to do when you want to do them!" Zig Ziglar

Really work on what we have begun thus far. Find yourself a really cool journal that you can love writing in each day forward. Give it an identification of some sort with your own creative markings and put your thoughts on paper about anything and everything you are thinking about since opening this book.

_____

_____

_____

_____

_____

_____

_____

_____

_____

_____

_____

_____

Action Step: (Spiritual Plane)

Really wanting to continue looking into your NOW? Trust where this
takes you (leaving the physical and mental planes) and write, write,
write in your real journal!

Personally, the exposure to a deeper understanding of Jesus, the Son of God, becoming human to show us the Father's love changed my life. My life in faith, my concepts of God, and my own self-worth were built upon the "should do" and "shouldn't dos" of fear and guilt. Spending time in prayer, in study, in quiet holiness became my greatest treasure. God absolutely cannot live without me! Jesus proves it. I need to remember when I lived with God, before I was born. I need to turn off the noise of this life and get back to God. The spark of everlasting love burns deeply in me, in you.

We have to spend time finding our God within. Seek and you shall find. Knock and it shall be opened unto you. It's true. When we stop, God is found. God is always there when we become aware. God is always there even when we are not aware. So what has to be done to become more aware of God's presence in our lives?

For me to become more aware, I know I have to listen, and I have to consciously and consistently spend time just looking around and purposefully becoming more aware. I mean, really looking.

God holds us in that very hand that created the universe and all that is—all created with love and purpose for you and for me, all created for us to find God, know God, and love God. We are given this life to understand the journey back to God and beyond self.

Life tends to get in the way of our journey back to God when it should be the way back to God. Our focus is the here and now. It has to be our focus too, or we couldn't become successful, self-sufficient members of society. The mystery within life calls us beyond the rules of here and now. Listening to my own "holy" becomes paramount after listening to God's whispers within.

Be still and listen. Look around too. God is screaming "I love you!" everywhere.

I understand that it isn't easy to *find my own holy* or realize that I've lost my "holy" within everything life is throwing at me. It seems that when times become the most overwhelming, I see myself struggling because I have lost sight of my flight-plan and helplessly crashed. Sometimes, the hardest realization is that there were passengers in my plane. My prayer is that our journey-time together will help you to avoid unnecessary learning-crashes and days of mourning.

Today is a Day of Mourning ~ Poem 5

Today is a day of mourning.
Today, I have chosen to weep for my own little child within.
I am sad because of all she has had to endure and sacrifice
To simply stay alive.
In spite of my learned knowledge,
My experiences of being free,
Creative
And filled with hope,
My private self has never been set free.
The realities I now face break my heart.
I am angry, confused,
Sad, tired.
I have been split in two for the last time.
I want out of my disenchanted forest,
This disillusional system that keeps dislodging my heart from my head.
How can I know of these needs to be creative,
Free
And happy;
Willing to risk
Yet, continue to hide my private self from my public self?
I cannot adapt to compensate,

Balance, enable
Or incorporate the public systems that breed
Control,
Dependency,
Stress
Or hopelessness any longer.

My son told me that he wished he was two again.
He is eleven years old and he already realizes
That his little boy has been crushed.
He already feels the pressures of being assigned
His roles in life.
He has already lost hope that the joy and freedom
We have shared thus far is gone.
My own little child outside myself causes me to mourn.
Life is difficult.
Joy must be found within.
This life's journey isn't just up to me.
If you risk nothing,
Then you risk everything.
Well, today is a day of mourning.
Today, I will weep
And then I will weep no more.

What would Jesus say to your inner child to help you feel better?

Action steps can help us to begin again.

Habits, prayer and planning can keep us on course to avoid regrets
and enable living fully in the NOW.

Letting Go of the Past ~ Poem 6

Standing alone at the top of a hill
I looked down at my world of tears.
I reached to heaven and gave up my will
With all my dysfunctional years.

Searching the sky for a perfect cloud
I found the one for me.
I cupped my hands and screamed out loud
"Take me into eternity!"

My perfect cloud came down from the sky
And I simply stepped inside.
The next thing I knew I was floating by
All the things I have tried to hide.

The higher my cloud went, the more I could see.
My whole life was before my eyes.
The truth that I faced was I haven't been me.
All the roles taken on were just lies.

I felt lighter than air when I touched the earth
With nothing else to be contrived.
Letting go of the past helps me see my own worth.
My true self really has survived!

"You cannot help but learn more as you take the world into your hands. Take it up reverently, for it is an old piece of clay, with millions of thumbprints on it." John Updike

"Make your faith larger than your fears and your dreams bigger than your doubts." Robin Sharma

"Learning life's lessons is not about making your life perfect, but about seeing life as it was meant to be." Elisabeth Kubler-Ross

Where is God? What is God saying? How can I master my physical plane?

God's Presence ~ Poem 7

God, creator of this earth of ours,
Uses pictures rich and clear.
God's love is seen in birds, in flowers.
God is trying to be near.

God, artist of our universe,
Paints colors in the sky.
We can see God's awesome love for us.
God, Creator, passing by.

It's not beyond our comprehension.
It is within our power to see,
God, father of creation,
Calling out to you and me.

Yes, the lover of humanity
Knew our lives were not complete.
So God sent the Son to set us free
And gave us victory through defeat.

May God, giver of the kingdom,
Fill your life in every way
With solutions to each problem
and God's presence every day.

God is within us and all around us. We need only to open ourselves and our awareness to Presence!
God is love. God took the initiative.

You are very blessed and deeply loved. Can you see how much God loves you? If you were the only person ever created, God would still have been Creator of All for just you. Bring in that awareness of blessings now, as I am speaking about the spiritual plane.

A blessing goes beyond the distinctions of admiration or love. It sees no virtue or vice, no good or evil. A blessing touches the original goodness of the other and calls forth belovedness.
Come and receive your blessing, God's beloved one.

A perfect place to end today's prayer!

Don't try too hard here.
Just be and let Jesus love you.

"What you celebrate expands." Danielle LaPorte

Action Step: (Physical Plane)

Rest in your blessing for 10 minutes. Do nothing. Say nothing.

Eye Opening Experience ~ Day 11 ~ Fully Invested

It is wonderful that you are here within the pages of this book and that God has this opportunity to share with you. You belong to God, and the world has you for just a little while. Your presence and love, your spirit and dedication, your *youness* is your precious joy. When you find things are overwhelming and the choices and responsibilities of living each day to the fullest seem to be too burdensome, pause to remember this humble blessing. This is the depth and the meaning in your life: God's calling of you in every moment, in every place.

Have you been one of the lucky ones?

Has your life been pretty awesome?

Are you a bit spoiled?

Have things been pretty difficult for you?

Have you been the one abused, misunderstood, disappointed, forgotten?

Within the good or the bad, is it still hard to say the word *yes* to anyone, much less to God?

"Don't ask of me, God. I don't want to die to self."

Perhaps it's time to trust in a God who loves you and to believe in the truth of blessings. This next song took me years to realize because I missed most of my childhood. Not sure how it happened, but I lived in unawareness. Never saw or understood the bigger picture. I grew up in Pittsburgh, Pennsylvania. The first time I came to Cleveland, Ohio, I was nineteen years of age, and I was shocked to discover that the rest of the world wasn't houses on the sides of hills, with water and bridges everywhere, like my little world at home. Cleveland was flat and spacious! I was astounded by the realization that I had heard many things but still structured everything within my narrow world of experiences.

If I was so naive about my physical world, imagine my surprise discovering the expansions of my spiritual world! The amazing perspective for me was realizing how much I was lacking and that I simply did not know it. I want to know. I want to choose. I want to say my yes with a greater depth of understanding. I want a bigger world, even as I fight and struggle with my selfish pride, my controlling ego, and the narrow visions of my tiny world of experiences.

I want to know a bigger God! I didn't always know that! I hope you know and hear God's call! I regret the no's but I celebrate my yes that has been my heart's delight for over 50 years now.

Don't forget! The link to listen to all my songs can be found at the bottom of each song sheet! **www.LivingInTheNowBook.com/music**

Speak To Me Of Life

♩=130

1. In the au-tumn of my life a gen - tle voice spoke___ to
2. In the mo-ments of my so - li - tude, God's voice comes back to
3. In the Son-shine of God's love for me, my words press on my
4. In the con - fi - dence of find - ing love, God's words burn___ my

1. me. You've got to lead___ My peo - ple now, you've got to set them
2. me. You've got to lead___ My pe - ple now, please help Me set them
3. mind. Help me un- - der-stand Your ways,___ Lord, I am so
4. heart. We share God's love___ and gen - tle peace by giv - ing love a

1. free. You've got to take the time right now to love them and to care. You'll
2. free.___ Walk for Me and talk for Me, I need your hu - man word. If
3. blind. I try to reach with o - pen hands, I want to live for You. I'll
4. start. We take the risk to love di - vine, we let God's Word be flesh. And

1. have to take the risk, My friend,___ they won't be - lieve I am___ there.
2. you won't give your-self for Me,___ My mes-sage will not be___ heard.
3. have to take the risk, my Friend,___ I must be - lieve love is___ true.
4. as we take in hu - man - kind,___ we e - cho our e - ter - nal yes.

REFRAIN

1. - 3.   No,   no,   no,   I   cried___   out.   No,   no,___
4.   Yes,   yes,   yes,   I   cry___   now.   Yes,   yes,___

1. - 3. no, I cried, not me.   Don't ask of me.
4.   yes, I cry, take me.   Ask love of me.

1. - 3. Oh, can't you see.___ I don't want to die___
4.   Now I can see.___ I shall live for You.   (Repeat refrain)

December 7, 1973 Words and Music by Patricia Jean Smithyman-Zito.

www.LivingInTheNowBook.com/music

I've come to learn of a man's story that I would like to share with you. His name is Mikey Robinson. He was involved in a serious plane crash, died on the hospital table, and then came back to life. He experienced leaving the physical plane, came to clearly understand the mental plane, and actually met God in the spiritual plane. You can read of his experiences by using the internet. For all practical purposes here, I will summarize his story, which I feel is a graphic illustration of becoming aware of the three planes we must encounter while learning to love ourselves, our world, and our journey back to God. Many people speak of near-death experiences and the profound changes impacting their lives as a result of the new perspectives they realize. I prefer learning this before I die!

Mickey Robinson was a skydiver who experienced a plane crash, and being on fire from head to toe after the crash, he ended up in a hospital with brain injuries, burns to a large portion of his body, and among other injuries, blindness in his right eye. He tells his story of being pulled from the plane, being rushed to the hospital, and actually dying as he lay on the hospital table. He speaks of seeing his spirit leave his physical body on the hospital table. As he says, "My inner man, the real me, my spirit sat up out of my body, and I could feel my legs go through the springs of the bed, and my spirit came out of my body as if you would take a glove off my hand. Instantly, I was in the spiritual world. I knew this was the real world! This man that I was seeing was the real me. Everything about the spiritual world is more real than this world . . . There is a complete absence of the awareness of time . . . Everything in the physical plane is relative to time . . . The spiritual plane is relative to eternity . . . I was totally conscious of eternity . . . No logic or reasoning was needed . . . You know what you know, what you know. I felt as if I were traveling . . . pulled to the compelling light . . . attracted to it . . . feeling the anticipation..."

Then I realized, off to my right, there was this blackness . . . something without any matter, any life. A void, where things were non-negotiable, cut off from the source of all life . . .

"It was horrific . . . It was so terrible you could never wish anyone, no matter how evil, to go there . . . It was a blackness that moved as I looked at it. The more it would sweep, it was eclipsing the light and closing in closer to me. I found myself standing on the very sliver edge, the precipice of eternal separation. 'I'm sorry! I want to live! Give me another chance!' my spirit screamed. Then I was in the presence of God Almighty. Instantly, I knew I would never die for eternity. This Being flowed as a river through my being. A golden radiation that was alive and going right through me filled my life with the experience of life, and I knew that this Being would take care of me for eternity. I found the love, majesty, authority flowing through me, and I was vibrating like a tuning fork within the essence of God's nature. Now with the knowledge of His purpose, I raced back through space and time and came to the room, waking and speaking a beautiful language. The blackness, I've since learned from God, was the darkness of my life of wrong choosing, and God gave me the space to cry out to Him."

Mikey Robinson's message to the world is that we need God and must choose God now, here in the physical and mental planes. We cannot wait until we are dying to make the decision to look God/Love in the face. It is precisely when we are experiencing pain or suffering, or a deep sadness that we must choose to use it to move more deeply into the spiritual plane, allowing God to flow through us as a river of life. We must learn to choose to die to self, right NOW. Choose to learn, listen, and experience life's flowing through each moment right here. Times of brokenness are the very times we are open enough and humble enough to see the inconsistencies and the disconnections (sin) in our journey through the three planes we try to participate in. I want to find the love, the majesty, the heart of God, and vibrate like a tuning fork, with the essence of God, for all to see. This gives meaning to life's challenging times and forces an awareness of living in the NOW.

"Before conversion, we tend to think of God as 'out there.' After transformation, we don't *look out at* reality as if it is hidden in the distance. We look *out from reality*! Our life is participating in God's Life. We are living in Christ." Fr. Richard Rohr, OFM

Write of your understanding of God. Write of your understanding of the 3 planes we are called to participate in as we continue our life-flight from here to eternity.

Think of examples in daily life or human experiences where there are strict regimens, focused behaviors, learned routines, language, clothing identifying a team, etc. that are not associated with religion. Do sports come to mind?

_____

_____

_____

_____

_____

_____

_____

_____

_____

_____

_____

_____

_____

_____

_____

_____

_____

_____

_____

_____

Action Step: (Mental Plane)

You can find more information about Mickey Robinson on the internet.

Google Mickey Robinson Extreme Prophetic.com.

Be Careful What You Wish For ~ Day 12 ~ God Knows Your Heart's Desire

Still the beginning:

When learning a new sport or another language, when purposefully replacing a habit or acquiring a new academic discipline, establishing the structure for creating new patterns may at first seem awkward. A formula is designed for learning skills, language, a short cut to a specific end.

Common to all these endeavors are progressive steps with measurable outcomes to show that I am learning. I know it is true when I see that I can actually do something new now. Aware of that, I want to suggest a structure that many have found to be very effective. You will of course, choose what works for you and what is most effective for you to see measurable outcomes each day.

Welcome to traveling your world with course corrections.

What are the aspirations of your heart? God knows. Do you? The language of God is in all the events of our own lives!

> I want to be a writer. I want to be a musician. I want to be a mystic.
> I want to be a faithful, selfless love-witness to God's people.
> I want to be the best daughter, sister, wife, mother, step-mom, grandma, aunt, cousin, Godmother, friend, servant on this earth. I want to be healthy. I want to be liked.
> I want…

Because God knows my heart's desires, my life demands more and changes radically when God intervenes. In the joys, in the surprises, in the demands, and in the disappointments God gets my attention and reminds me of my true self and my true visions/my heart's desires…these are what I lovingly refer to as my "appointed times" and they can be rough!

Would I have had those desires, loves and even disappointments if my course corrections were not empowered by my relationship with God? The answer is yes, but where is the inner peace, the happiness and the joy of the journey? Oh, yeah, God is in charge and that's where I find a deeper meaning!

Suffer - Poem ~ 8

This is the holy of holy times.
It is the sacred time of Lent.
Can you tell me why we force ourselves to
suffer the endless sufferings of discipline?
Within every moment that I live
I believe that I am walking the walk.
Yet, within a matter of moments, I realize that
I am as weak as I have ever been.

No matter how hard I try
the most obvious conclusions that come to me
are always that I am as humbled and small as ever.
I cannot tell you of my fears, my deep regrets.
I am as weak as any have ever been.
Where, oh, where are all the graces and
all the blessings that I have believed in
all the days of my life that have made me "ME"?

I really cannot believe I am holy and it's
because I can't quite figure God's love.
In a world where nothing is true
how is it that the Word is forever?

Many people touch my life
and enable me to stand in the presence of God.
Yet, there are still those insane moments
when absolutely nothing follows any of the rules.

If I am holy and strong, I can make choices
that keep me in God's grace.
Today is the day I make a choice
to humbly stay close to my loving God.
This is a very holy season.
It is a time for me to turn
my life around within God's grace.
Help me, oh God, for I am a sinner.

I think we try too hard! Mother Theresa spent most of her religious life doubting the existence of God but she loved and served faithfully anyway.

The Woman Who Tried to Climb the Lake

Once there was a woman who spent her whole life climbing a very high mountain. She began as a tiny child, and could not remember a time before the mountain. Year after year she would ascend the steep cliffs, and in the process she became very good at the motion of climbing. The muscles in her legs and her back grew strong, and after a while, climbing felt as natural to her as breathing. As time passed, and she went higher and higher, she didn't even have to try and climb anymore-her body did it automatically.

At last, one day, the woman reached the top of the mountain. She was overjoyed with her achievement, and couldn't wait to start out on the next portion of her travels, and to conquer her next mountain. As she looked out over the horizon, she saw a beautiful blue lake, stretching sideways as far as her eye could see. But being a climber all of her life, the woman had only lived on the mountains, so she had never seen a lake, and in fact, did not even know what a lake was.

She watched the strange expanse before her, and concluded that it must be some unusual kind of "blue" mountain. Since the only way to continue her journey was to cross over the odd-looking blue form, she decided that was what she must do.

So the mountain woman walked up to the water, and began trying to "climb the lake" with the same motions she'd used to climb the mountain. At first, she couldn't understand why she wasn't making any progress, and in fact, was exhausting herself. So she mustered all of the energy in her strong body and tried to "climb" even harder, placing one leg in front of the other, using her hands to attempt to grasp the "blue rocks." But her efforts were useless. She kept falling over, and wasn't going anywhere.

Just about this time, when the mountain woman felt like giving up, she noticed a person floating by on top of the blue lake, gently gliding his body through the water with the slightest movements of his arms and legs.

"What are you doing, my friend?" he called out to her.
"What does it look like?" she answered, her face flustered with embarrassment. "I'm climbing."
"Good woman," the man of the lake replied, "don't you know that you can't cross a lake by climbing it? The only way to travel through water is to swim."
"But I'm such a marvelous climber!" the mountain woman insisted. "I've spent my whole life learning to climb. I can climb any mountain, I can reach any peak. Surely there must be some way I can climb the lake."

"I'm sure you are an excellent climber," the man of the lake answered politely. "But that skill won't help you here in the water. It took one kind of wisdom to get you to the top of the mountain-you had to make your power stronger than the mountain. Now you need to learn another kind of wisdom to get across the lake-you need to surrender to the power of the water and allow its force to be stronger than you.

You don't have to try hard anymore. In fact, the less you try, the better you'll do!"

And so it was that the man of the lake taught the woman of the mountain how to swim. At first, she splashed and thrashed around in the water, for she was accustomed to using very strong energy in her climbing. But her teacher was very patient, and slowly she learned to float on the water's surface, and allow the waves and the wind to carry her gently forward, until she was hardly doing anything at all.

And that's how the mountain woman learned that the strength of surrender was just as powerful as the strength of pushing forward. (Author Unknown)

Rest in the Lord, and wait patiently for Him. (Psalm 37:7)

Those who wait for the Lord shall renew their strength, they shall mount up with wings like eagles, they shall run and not be weary, they shall walk and not faint. (Isaiah 40:31)

Without a dream to light your way, the world is a very dark place." Marrion Zimmer Bradley

Write of the aspirations of your heart.

What does it mean that the language of God is in all the events of our own lives?

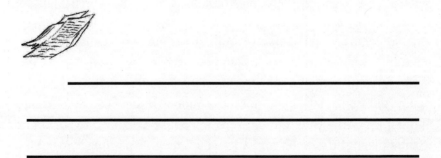

_____

_____

_____

_____

_____

_____

_____

_____

_____

_____

_____

_____

Action Step: (Spiritual Plane)

Write about what your true self desires once your physical plane and
mental plane get out of the way.

Every moment is really like a new day! Let's begin today's journey with a song in our hearts!

October 15, 2001 Words and Music by Patricia Jean Smithyman-Zito.

www.LivingInTheNowBook.com/music

We are loved with an everlasting love and called to a holiness that transcends everything. You are actively pursuing this blessedness, and God is proud of you. This affirmation of your true self reclaims you, and it will center you in the arms of your God who has always been there waiting.

None of us will ever be allowed to live this life alone. We can choose to be more aware. We can decide to work at becoming holy, happy, and eager to love in the holy abundance of every new moment. To make such a choice is to acknowledge that we are special. You are special, and I am extending my hand in a blessing that comes from everywhere, but from the soul it gets its start. Its source is far beyond me. I bring you this gift as a messenger. It is not from me, but I totally participate in extending it to you.

We need to be aware of expanding our thinking beyond self. I pray for blessings and grace because I want to try to open my mind, my heart, my world. The expansion of who I am is a surrendering. Oftentimes, it is suffering that bends us into surrender, and it becomes a forced learning of acceptance. It is very hard to change how we look at things. I want to understand that veritable pause of true surrender in a busy life that enables us to see more, the reasons why, the gift of living in this holy, abundant NOW without negative factors, such as illness, death, unemployment, divorce, etc., forcing us into pause, ponder, and change. It is possible to make life real. I just took a major part of my lifetime to grasp that.

A Masterpiece ~ Poem 9

As a simple composer, I can musically appeal to you,
stirring emotions, needs, and images
you often try not to address or focus on.

As an honest writer, I can quietly approach you,
proving with words that you have not
always appreciated your gifts and blessings.

As a positive teacher, I can raise thoughts and questions for you,
enabling you to preface each moment
with great awareness, deep gratitude, and honest love.

As a genuine person, I can share my celebrations of life and love
with you,
watching as you hear, see, smell, taste, and touch
the peaks and abysses of being real.

As a companion on the journey, I can focus on this fragmented
masterpiece of you,
learning of love as God touches your soul and moves your heart to
grasp life's miracles in you.

Composer, writer, teacher, and genuine person, yes, but to be a
companion on the journey with you is awesome! You can reach
into my journey, and I can reach into your journey. Without actual
physical communication, we will be present to each other.

There are no positive or negative responses, no judgment being made,
not even an opinion or point of view.

The blessings that we give to each other are expressions of the blessing
that rests within us from all eternity. It is the deepest affirmation of
our true self. Good words are being spoken to you and about you—
words that speak to you of your own truth. Yes, I have a gift for you.
Yes, I need your gift for me too.

"You don't have to be what other people want you to be. You don't
have to be interesting or agreeable or entertaining. You don't have
to tone yourself down, quiet your voice, or hide your feelings. You
don't have to be outgoing or spontaneous or sociable. You don't have
to be thin or beautiful or anyone's definition of attractive. You don't
have to be anyone other than who you authentically are, and you sure
as hell don't have to spend your time and energy trying to convince

people that you're worth keeping around. The right people are going to recognize your worth. They are going to respect you, appreciate you, and accept you, without forcing you to compromise who you are. Life is too short, and your happiness is far too important, to make room for anyone who treats you otherwise." Daniell Keopke

What does this connection of becoming companions on the journey mean to you?

Explain how we can be a blessing to others without actually being in their presence or speaking with them.

Try praying for every person who has ever worked on your car!

Can we be the person who always shows up and does a good job?

Do I bless the people before me each day? Do I say thank-you? Do I notice people doing the right thing?

_____

_____

_____

_____

_____

_____

_____

_____

_____

_____

_____

_____

_____

_____

_____

_____

_____

_____

Action Step: (Physical Plane)

What is it you wish to know more about? Has your vision and understanding of the physical plane expanded here?

Risk ~ Day 14 ~ Openness

Today we have a fable/story about the benefits of an open mind!

Melvin Marsh Wren argued against new ideas until his friends found great success by embracing a satisfying new adventure while he just went hungry.

Bonnie and Benny, Blue Herons, liked to explore new things and places. They recently heard about how cattail plants were growing in Mellow Marsh. They decided to invite their friends, Molly and Melvin—both Marsh Wrens—to accompany them to the Marsh. Molly squealed, "I'd love to go, especially when cattails are in bloom!" Melvin looked suspiciously at his friends. "It's great right here at Paradise Pond. Why go all the way over to the Marsh? We've got plenty of mosquitoes to eat in our own backyard."

"It'll be fun and I want to enjoy the weather and chat along the way. I'm sure we'll find something to eat at the Marsh," explained Molly encouragingly. "I agree," Benny replied. "Who knows what we'll find on such an adventure?"

Molly said, "Come on, Melvin. It'll be fantastic!"

Melvin harrumphed. "No thanks, I'm staying here where the water's nice and lunch is nearby."

Bonnie, Benny, and Molly headed for Mellow Marsh. Upon arrival, they couldn't believe their eyes! The mosquitoes swarmed everywhere and marsh grasses clumped perfectly for perching. They stuffed themselves and then perched to watch the world go by. They made several new friends, too. It was heavenly!

When they got home, Melvin asked, "What took so long?" "Oh, Melvin, Mellow Marsh was wonderful!" Molly gasped. "We ate and watched the Marsh activity and then we ate again. Millions of tender mosquitoes surrounded us! We made new friends, too!" Melvin sighed. "I only caught 3 mosquitoes the whole time! I'm going on the next adventure," Melvin said as his stomach growled.

Today's course correction to ponder and implement: Keep an open mind and you will thrive.

Melvin the Marsh Wren wasn't open to new places and things. He wasn't interested in visiting Mellow Marsh. But his friends, Bonnie and Benny, the Blue Herons, loved to explore. Melvin's friend, Molly the Marsh Wren was excited to experience an adventure to Mellow Marsh. Bonnie, Benny, and Molly delighted in the unknown possibilities of a trip to the Marsh.

They were open-minded and looked forward excitedly to the prospects the Marsh might offer. As expected, they found an adventure that lived up to its possibilities. Even when his friends encouraged him, Melvin refused to accompany them. Melvin believed that what he had at home was better than what he would find at Mellow Marsh. He thought it was a hassle to travel to the Marsh. Melvin's mind was closed to new adventures. Melvin was quite disappointed when he heard Molly's stories of plentiful food at the Marsh. He saw their full bellies and heard interesting tales about their adventure.

Some days I'm like Melvin and not comfortable with new situations, not willing to venture out of my comfort zone. This closed mind drastically limits all the possibilities in my NOW!

Sometimes, I am more like Molly, and easily embrace the opportunities in my life that come along. I just seem to have an open mind. With course corrections, I'm willing to try new things, to risk, and I find that my NOW is thriving.

When your mind is open to everything, you're more likely to enjoy a thriving, fascinating life!

Self-Reflection Questions:

1. Do you have an open mind?
2. How do you feel when a new opportunity comes along?
3. What more can you do to take full advantage of all that life offers?

A Gift for You ~ Poem 10

I have a gift for you,
Although it isn't quite from me.
I give it to you from my heart.
It's as simple as a gift can be.

It comes from everywhere,
But from the soul, it gets its start.
I pray that you'll be open now.
This benison is from my heart.

Benison means "blessing,"
Like a formal benediction.
Concentrate and be present now,
For I pray with great conviction.

May you know that you are loved.
May every breath you take bear out
The many blessings you possess
To take away your fear and doubt.

May God Almighty be
Within your heart, within your soul,
And give you everything you need
To trust God's absolute control.

Claim your benison, your blessing, in all its simplicity. God helps those who help themselves. I come to remind you of all your blessings. When we place ourselves before the Lord and ponder all He does, we will touch, see, and hear the blessings surrounding us, creating a grateful heart.

I am grateful you are here. Thank you for blessing my life! Know that you are prayed for to:

Step fully into your NOW and be present on purpose.
Welcome everything and everyone as your gift.
Focus on blessings in the middle of all things.

What blessing are you most aware of right now?

What steps must be taken to realize the bigger picture?

What areas of your living are expansive, completely understood, filled with wisdom and grace?

Write a bit about your gifts, talents, and treasures and how you can or do share.

_____

_____

_____

_____

_____

_____

_____

_____

_____

_____

_____

_____

_____

_____

_____

_____

_____

Action Step: (Mental Plane)

"Purpose is the thread that connects the dots to everything you do that leads you to an extraordinary life." Oprah Winfrey

What has changed in how you see things and think of things?

<u>My, My, My ~ Poem 11</u>

My struggle: understanding life's meanings within stress.
My goal: knowing self enough to become more by living with less.

My silence: a barrier to communication.
My unhappiness: a result of some type of victimization.

My solitude: thought of as a form of self-protection.
My confusions: living life without depth and moving in every direction.

My efforts: lifting the burdens that I bear.
My words: that finally, I choose to share.

My hope: that in the truth I am alive.
My dream: I really can and will survive.

Radical change can and will occur. We do not have to "go" anywhere. This radical change of which I speak is the change from living life as a painful test to prove that we deserve to be loved and respected to living it as an unceasing *yes* to the *truth* of our belovedness. In spite of all my limitations, beyond all my failings, within me, God moves and breathes and brings life's spark of wonder and grace. God desires union.

<u>"Drop the Rocks!"</u> by Patricia Ann Smith, OP

Struggling down the road holding tight to my sack,
I stopped under a tree to rest and Jesus was there.
He said, "Drop the rocks!"
I looked long at the sack and thought, "I can't!"
His smile said, "You can!"

I said to him:

"But, I don't want to forgive them." Jesus said, "Drop the rocks!"

"But they didn't accept me!" Jesus said, "Drop the rocks!"

"I think they didn't believe me!" Jesus said, "Drop the rocks!"

"I was so hurt!" Jesus said, "Drop the rocks!"

"I have a lot of anger still!" Jesus said, "Drop the rocks!"

"I feel like a failure!" Jesus said, "Drop the rocks!"

"What if they can't forgive me?" Jesus said, "Drop the rocks!"

"What if it happens again?" Jesus said, "Drop the rocks!"

"But this is so hard!" Jesus said, "Drop the rocks!"

"What about them?" Jesus said, "Drop the rocks!"

"I feel so alone." Jesus said, "Drop the rocks!"

"You are never alone.

I love you and am always with you no matter what.

Now, empty the sack."

In a wash of tears, I emptied the sack and started to fold it.

Jesus said, "Burn the sack. The only rocks you can carry now

are the few little ones you gather on the way each day,

and you must carry these in your shoes!"

Every night drop the rocks into eternity and begin anew."

I said, "Okay, Lord!"

And, taking just myself, I continued my journey...

lighter, freer, refreshed!

Life is a God-given opportunity to become who we are, to affirm our true spiritual self, to claim our beautiful truth, and to appropriate and integrate the realities of our being. Most of all, it is a journey to say yes to the One who calls us beloved and who blesses us constantly. God has been calling for a long time. Listen for your blessings, as I listen for mine. We will know who we are and see all we are called to be. It is a wonderful awareness to share.

Isn't it amazing that as I put my physical plane into purposeful structure I find my aura, my pure field of energy surrounding my body, to mirror my soul and attract the universal God force to me?

Just stop and think for a while. Listen for God's words of blessing and rest in love's call.

Amen.

Insecure? Take vitamin I
"In Him who is the source of my strength I have strength for everything." Philippians 4:13

_____

_____

_____

_____

_____

_____

_____

_____

_____

_____

_____

———————————————————

———————————————————

———————————————————

———————————————————

———————————————————

———————————————————

———————————————————

———————————————————

———————————————————

———————————————————

Action Step: (Spiritual Plane)

Every living thing has an aura, a power source of energy. Stretch your mind to become more aware of your senses. See your senses from the inside and, mind alert, reach out with that part of your mind that desires knowledge to start shaping and using your energy field's power within your NOW.

A Bit of Heaven

September 5, 1975 Words and Music by Patricia Jean Smithyman-Zito.

www.LivingInTheNowBook.com/music

One interesting point to focus on today is that Jesus was sent to earth. We have been sent to earth. Jesus came to do the will of His Father. We grow in grace and wisdom, just as Jesus did, to know and live the Father's will for us. Jesus didn't decide to come to earth any more than you or I did. Or could it be that Jesus's unconditional love was the only choice needed? We find ourselves here trying to know God, as God knows, before our times to choose are up. We are companions on the journey—the journey of a lifetime! Sent to earth, we must come to see the beauty in one another and in the world in which we live. God desires union.

All My Life ~ Poem 12

You speak of miracles, love overflowing,
the promise of gifts divine.
Yet, all my life I've searched outside,
feeling happiness could never be mine.

You speak of treasures, creativeness showing,
the wonders of life sublime.
But, all my life I've reached beyond me,
longing for the freedom I never could find.

You speak of humanity, gentleness, touching.
God's Son exploding through time.
So, all my life I've prayed intensely,
believing that love would be my sign.

You speak of presence, silence and strength,
my soul, my heart, my mind.
And, all my life I've journeyed in Spirit,
trusting transformation would birth love denied.

You speak of power, ecstasy, peace.
Potentials of self, defined.

Still, all my life I've struggled within,
to see weakness and strength combined.

Now I speak of happiness, freedom and loving,
transformation of self through time.
I guess all my life I've tried to keep growing,
dropping masks and all pantomime.

Yes, speak to me, walk with me, teach me.
My person no longer denied.
All my life, I've searched outside myself,
for that person you've shown me I am inside.

"Death and fear of the unknown can be seen in our apparent loss of
direction, the disappearance of signposts, of ways which previously
we took to be methods of advancing."
Fr. Michael Hollings

<u>My Worth ~ Poem 13</u>

I am the role that I must procure, the journey I must go.
I am the suffering I endure and only I need know.

I am the good that love portrays and the dance I long to try.
I am the security within my days where I allow faith to abide.

I am the time in a chosen day, the alleluia ringing clear.
I am new life and love's hooray if only I pause to hear.

I am the song that I long to sing, the Word made flesh through me.
I am the peace I now can bring to everyone I see.

I am the sum of the love I receive, the echo of God on earth.
I am as precious as I can be. God's love gives me my worth.

Be that person of integrity and be that "someone."
Pick up the paper towels all over the bathroom floor when everyone
says "someone" will pick it up.

Be the "someone," precious, proud and able to listen when the vet
can't find food by inviting him/her home for a shower and a meal.
"Someone" will let that car cut into the traffic lane with a nod and a
smile instead of a gesture.

Believing Each Day ~ Poem 14

The finger of God has written
Words of love in my heart.
But my power of recollection
Requires more than grace to start.
My personhood must tread on the earth
And on the flesh to grow.
Beyond the gain of human worth
So the image and likeness of God can show.

Well, are there people in your life who see who you are inside and
show you who you are inside?
Is there someone with whom you have discovered life's meaning?

How can we be open enough to speak of *happiness, freedom, and
loving, transformation of self* through time? How can we actually
hear when someone is speaking of God or our need to change?

_____

_____

_____

_____

_____

_____

_____

_____

_____

_____

_____

_____

_____

Action Step: (Physical Plane)

What is God's plan for you really about and how are you tapping resources and people to uncover your true NOW?

Soon another Feast came around and Jesus was back in Jerusalem. Near the Sheep Gate in Jerusalem there was a pool, in Hebrew called Bethesda, with five alcoves. Hundreds of sick people—blind, crippled, paralyzed—were in these alcoves. One man had been an invalid there for thirty-eight years. When Jesus saw him stretched out by the pool and knew how long he had been there, He said, "Do you want to get well?" The sick man said, "Sir, when the water is stirred, I don't have anybody to put me in the pool. By the time I get there, somebody else is already in." Jesus said, "Get up, take your bedroll, and start walking." The man was healed on the spot. He picked up his bedroll and walked off. (John 5:1–9)

So the story says that the angel went down at a certain season into the pool and troubled the water. Whoever was first to step in, after the troubling of the water, was made whole of whatever disease or inner struggle that crippled their growth to live life more fully. Reading this passage for the hundredth time, it is suddenly saying something very different to me. For years, I have searched for God in the troubled waters of my life. I think I learned, very early in life, that God was constantly sending angels to stir the waters to bring my attention back to God. I believe I was always trying to be attentive to the holy moments of awareness in my life. Being a "doer," I was not sleeping by the side of the pool! My problem was that I believed that the deepest places of my inner self could only be found when the waters were troubled. I believed that I could never be really happy or satisfied in this life because we were meant to "become more," and that was basically forced upon us in the sad and troubled moments of our lives. That was what made us grow. Now I see that my life is taking on new and more involved perspectives.

I choose to no longer focus on the troubled waters. Life and its beauty now take me beyond that former, inward, and kind of selfish perspective. I've grown enough to know that I can control many things. Now I choose to look up. I want to focus on that angel! Wholeness is within me first. God is my focus. Most of my seasons within are beautiful.

Your yes cannot be spoken by anyone else at any moment. Nobody can give God your praise and honor in this moment. Nobody can speak your kindnesses, share your heart's love, or be present in your NOW. Don't miss the golden, holy opportunity to sing God's glory and to love in this gift of holy, abundant NOW! Even in my yes, I missed many holy moments.

"No matter what emptiness you feel, no matter how great your suffering in mind or body, no matter what anxiety or joy you have, no matter how wretched or desolate you may be, remember the words of Jesus: I will be there." Fr. Michael Hollings

Ponder what cripples you, blinds you, and stops you from picking up your bedroll and walking away from that which is not your best.

Who shall you speak to of this?
Have you been waiting by the waters long enough?
Can you hear your whispered *yes*?
Can your yes wrap around new perspectives?

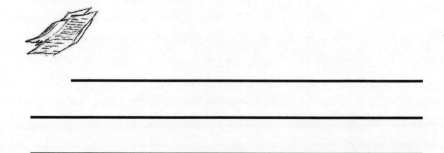

Action Step: (Mental Plane)

Get moving and tap into your plans of power plotted out thus far on your journey. Check and double check your physical plane plans to perfect their purposes of change to help your mind and your thoughts stay focused.

We prepare and practice to compete for running a race and expect to have pain. Suffering is more about falling during the race and not being able to finish! Suffering is the emotional attachment to pain. When a loved one dies, we feel the pain of loss but we know they are free of suffering.

Both events are within the physical plane but my mental plane has to label suffering, pain, tests and experiences to take everything to a higher level. They are like drills!

<u>Our Test ~ Poem 15</u>

So many people no matter where we turn.
Why must we suffer? What is it we must learn?

So many problems everywhere we go.
Where are all the answers? What are we supposed to know?

There are so many pressures from every avenue.
When will it ever end? Please stop, I'm asking you!

All of us are busy doing things that must be done.
We go and go and go and go. Has anyone ever won?

I think it's time to stop now and analyze this fact.
That once the moment passes by we cannot get it back.

So pause and ponder what is NOW and how to use time best.
Each moment is a miracle and loving life, our test.

Never Ending Journey ~ Poem 16

For as much as my heart
Searches for my soul,
For as often as I've had a new start
Determined to find my self-control,
Wouldn't you agree
That by now
My spirit would be free?

No matter where I begin
My pursuit towards perfection,
I simply cannot win
The prize of peace in my reflection.
Yet, it would seem to me
That somehow
My spirit should be free.

Oh, I shall continue
On my never ending journey
To Your all elusive presence, God, to You.
In seeking You, I know I will find me.
Only then, I see,
Will my journey allow
My spirit to be free.

I Seek God's Presence ~ Poem 17

Alone with God, my most welcomed Guest,
Love comes when I take time to rest.

In that solitude of quiet time,
Answers of the heart are quite sublime.

I seek God's presence in an inner room,
Where I'm free from worry, stress or gloom.

God's special blessings bestowed on me,
I pray for love, happiness, tranquility.

A lot to ask for, this I know,
But seek and find, God tells us so.

The longer I live, the deeper my prayer,
The greater the day, the more I can share.

I Play in the Day I'm In ~ Poem 18

Beaten down, battered, broken, afraid,
Will pain go away if I'm strong?
While tears flow copiously, I have prayed
That weeping can't be wrong.

Understanding, attentive, patient, and real,
You reach out and I'm alive.
Again tears flow freely as I truly feel,
And I'm ready to survive.

Breaking veritable walls of darkness,
Cautiously backing away to see,
Assembling all truth I sincerely confess
In this day I can be free.

Who knows the reasons or who is to say
Why we go through what we must?
It's taking each moment as gift for today
That helps us grow in love and trust.

So now I play in the day I'm in,
As productive as I can be.
Living here, loving NOW is how I win
And keep life alive for me.

<u>Okay ~ Poem 19</u>

When all the things that I believe
In seem to fall apart,
When things I'm trying to perceive
Construe to break my heart,
When hope dissolves to deep despair
And joy cannot be found,
I join in quiet times of prayer
To turn it all around.
But if it be that I must lose
These battles that I wage,
Help me win the war and choose
The things You whisper through each stage.
Perhaps, indeed, through each new phase
I'm learning how to be
A servant who can sing God's praise,
With or without a symphony.
So instead of asking, as I pray
For what I seem to think I need,
Consume me as You must, okay.
I'm ready to proceed.

Oh, God, Make Haste!

March 14, 2011 Words and Music by Patricia Jean Smithyman-Zito.

www.LivingInTheNowBook.com/music

"Tomorrow's illiterate will not be the man who can't read; he will be the man who has not learned how to learn." Herbert Gerjuoy

Re-read today's poems of struggle and note how they move into awareness and trust in the end.

Ideally, we should begin each moment with an established awareness of prosperity and abundance to be open to new sources and channels of consciousness to better receive all that is good, NOW.

I need to know that so as not to crumble within my pendulum-swinging struggle of seeking. I must learn to trust myself and trust life for all to be well. What or who brings equilibrium back into your NOW?

_____

_____

_____

_____

_____

_____

_____

_____

Action Step: (Spiritual Plane)

Aware of mastering the physical plane with structure and habits, I can align my mental plane to the positive powers of progress in my NOW. Spend time in the overflow of abundance you've discovered using prayer, meditation and quiet that will always transport you into presence and holiness.

The View ~ Day 19 ~ The Truth

On a cold February morning, when temperatures had been around five or six degrees outside for weeks, I was shivering and becoming quite tired of winter. The next day it was thirty-two degrees. Thirty-two degrees was good! Wait a minute, that's freezing! Considering where the temperatures had been in the low single digits, thirty-two degrees felt warm!

Perspective changes one's point of view.

As I came up a small crest in the road by my home and crossed over the short bridge spanning the Chagrin River, I came upon this blanket of white fog, with the sun shining through it. I drove through this low cloud, and I heard God say, "My love is always with you. Even in the cold, bitter times. The sun will shine, the clouds will dissipate, temperatures will go up, and everything will bloom again. My blanket of love is visible."

There will be many surprises and reassurances to see within the cold and cloudy days of life. We must put on our coat, hat, and gloves and allow God to be present in our lives.

Doing what we need to do "outside of ourselves" can give us the opportunity to see, feel, and hear God if we but stop to ponder.

The cloud that went across the road was breathtaking. Six more weeks of winter will be okay.

The little cloud across the road was not the destination. It was a gift of beauty in the middle of my winter journey.

There's a blanket of God's life warming my heart, giving my spirit hope, and taking my mind to the depths of contemplation that I desperately need. You do too! We simply must get up and get moving and take on life, allowing God to move, to shine. Stepping up to truth again is the place to start. Somehow, in looking at our truth, we come to know what to do for everything because we know God is in control and Son-shine is ours always.

Here's an eye-opening suggestion from a very unexpected source: Watch the Disney movie, Pollyanna, with Hayley Mills, and take note of the infectious perception of life portrayed. This is a profound paradigm shift that will cause you to question what lens you use as you view life.

"Challenges are what make life interesting. Overcoming them is what makes life meaningful." Joshua J. Marine

"You don't drown by falling in the water; you drown by staying there." Ed Cole

How much are you really seeing within each moment of your gifted NOW?

Are you overwhelmed in awareness of how God loves you? Has the physical plane become your resource for God-moments since you have spent almost 20 days understanding everything differently?

Is there a movie you've seen or an event in history you can recall that confirms the awareness that any response to any event can change you completely?

Share your new view of discovering this gift of your abundant truth.

_____

_____

_____

_____

_____

_____

_____

_____

_____

_____

Action Step: (Physical Plane)

Try to watch the Disney movie, Pollyanna, with Hayley Mills.

Check over your choices of forming daily habits to hold yourself accountable and to discern the growing benefits from your self-discipline.

Mindfulness ~ Day 20 ~ No More Should or Have To

Are you living a life that is performance based? If most of your focus is in the physical world, then you are. It is hard to live a life that is heart-directed or goal-directed in the spiritual sense, because the world we move and breathe and live in is concrete, tangible, and within the limits of our senses. Focusing away from what society drills into our heads about success gives us permission to dream and to choose simple goals providing pleasure or peace or hope and are necessary releases to keep us from burning out. Disappointments, stresses and pressures are inevitable.

Perspectives need to change. We need to stop and take a good look at the source, the motivation, and the necessities of our thinking, our planning and our goal setting.

I speak of life's 3 planes of awareness. The physical, mental and spiritual planes should keep us grounded and aware in different ways. Forgetting all the programmed data we've been fed throughout our lives, we are learning how to target each plane and become more aware of seeing our NOW differently. (Being and living fully so each day is our best!)

The 3 planes of awareness we have been looking into create a synergy bringing us to mindfulness living in the *NOW.*

Why is this important? Because it is in this state of mindfulness that the box is more than a box, and a song is more than harmonious melody. Because I can meet/find/be aware of God in my every NOW. The day is more than just another rat-race day. Even in the rat race, while living in this mindfulness, events are seen as the gifts and songs they are intended for each of us, by God, who says, ***"This is all composed for you."***

The materials or tools offered for aids in this growth of awareness journey of life itself are not new. We can liken this to having eggs, flour, cream and salt on the counter or in a bowl to make crepes, Irish soda bread or Belgian waffles. The differences in the outcomes are determined by the recipe and the skill of the cook/chef. Everyone recognizes the ingredients. What determines the menu for the meal? What determines the day's gifts being revealed? It's all determined by the chef. It is all determined by one's mindfulness and purpose.

Ask yourself when and where you passed through a cold and cloudy experience as I described in yesterday's story. Were you aware, mindful and able to find a deeper meaning to that physical plane experience? As seen today, you can turn the things that you think about into things that you can see, touch, taste, smell, hear and appreciate. We all have the ingredients for putting something awesome together but my meal and Chef Brandon's meal are light years apart! In other words, you can turn your focused thoughts into reality and benefit greatly with purpose and direction.

We all have the same brain hardware. Everyone operates with the raw processing mental powers. What separates us is the software choices we make and the self-awareness we use to support our mind so it is working for us instead of against us. Spend time in prayer to stop shaping your world according to should or have to and focus on freeing your brain to work the creative way you want it to work. Empty enough to go where your brain takes you, where your heart leans, where your soul longs to inspire you through meditation.

"When I let go of what I am, I become what I might be." Lao Tzu

Write about it here and ponder how God longs to be present in it all.

_____

_____

_____

_____

_____

_____

_____

_____

Trying to keep on trying?

Take vitamin T. "Trust in the Lord with all your heart, on your own intelligence rely not; in all your ways be mindful of Him, and He will make straight your paths." Proverbs 3:5-6

"The concrete, the specific, the physical, the here-and-now, when we can be present to it in all of its ordinariness, becomes the gateway to the Eternal." Richard Rohr, OFM

Action Step: (Mental Plane)

Spend quiet time within each of the 3 planes of awareness and become more aware of how your focused thoughts and actions weave meaning into your NOW. This is also a good time to check on how you are progressing within all your changes. You may find it helpful to go back to *Journal Work ~ Day 5 ~ Exchange Between Planes.*

"Becoming more" requires awareness. I truly must look for the truth in everything. I'm trying now to see life as it really is—that is, as God sees it—instead of seeing everything as I think it is or as I wish it could be.

Prayer provides a platform enabling us to participate more fully in our truth. All that we experience in our lives can open us to wisdom and transformation. Learning to love and understand, beyond self is "becoming more" and brings peace and happiness beyond measure. It doesn't come without a price. Suffering and disappointment, bringing us to our knees, can be a necessary motivation to become more open, to acknowledge our need for others, and to expand our trust. It is within crisis that we are forced to stop. There and then we notice. Everything becomes as it is; real. Now, our world is not so much as we've been thinking everything is around us. It is within the chaos of crisis that we are softened enough to let the world, others and God come in.

Significant others can reflect the truth of our NOW back to us when we have been forced to stop within the chaos of our physical and mental planes. While we are speaking of significant others who participate in the physical world with us, I want to address the realities of dying. We tend to not want to talk about it with any depth, especially when someone you love passes away. There should be a whisper in the wind, some kind of a warning sign, to help prepare for those cold and windy days of darkness and disappointment. Avoidance isn't the best way to live life or face death. We can't prepare for death's actual moment, although it is coming for all of us, and we know it. We can fix our mind and prepare our heart, but we still cannot help but react when death happens. There's a type of violence in the separation. It's the mystery, the chasm, the disconnection, the lost truth we have to live through. We don't really know about it or understand it, although we all have to experience it. When in the middle of someone's dying, there's nothing more important to do but be there.

I want to touch on leaving the physical plane and share my own ways of putting some kind of structure to the chaos. Naming the emotions and walking a path that can guide us through the thinking and feeling are the processes. Growing around an understanding of what has to happen beforehand will help to ease the sorrow, eliminate the fear, and lessen the pain found within moving through life's realities to the other side. This process of thinking goes into the woods with us to help us see the forest from the trees. No one can go into the forest for us or even with us.

This section of the book provides a type of perspective and loving support. I hope you will work with this perspective, regardless of having had the experience of loss or not.

Everyone asks if there is anything they can do for us during a time of loss. We receive cards, phone calls, pots of chili, spaghetti sauce, or flowers or tokens of "I wish I could help you" or "I'm so sorry for your loss" expressions. There is a whisper in the wind. There always has been. It's that state of emptiness. It allows us to be cognizant, to be open, to become more aware of the bridge between the physical world we live in with all the noise and chaos that extends over the gap into the spiritual world that is truly all around us. The whisper in the wind will lead us.

There may be a friend's words, a scripture passage, or the beginnings of a meditation, a poem or a song that will provide multi-emotional involvement. Some people need auditory stimuli, like a song or someone's kind words, to be reached. Some people use visual aids to truly *see* everything more clearly, like a poster made of pictures. I think everyone can benefit from the kinesthetic hands-on beauties and perspectives of coming to understand there is a world deep inside each of us. Everyone walks and talks in the physical world. We need to walk and talk in the spiritual world too.

This section of the book will move through what is outside of us all and help us focus inside, where there is a whole other world waiting for us. Deep inside, we can find our light, our energy source, our center of strength. Down inside, we can journey into a world greater than the physical world we know, live in, and walk in right now. Down inside, in our soul, in the depths of our inner spirit world, we can tap resources to know and understand, to feel, and to speak within our own truth.

Let's visualize doors that we may open, deep inside our true self, to meet truth, love, and peace, shall we?

Let's close our eyes and settle our body. Breathing more slowly, let's become aware of slowing down and actually focusing on the long, deep, purposeful, calming breath. Let's use our mind to quiet our body and use our body to quiet our mind. This takes time, and it is something we must always practice doing. When ready, let's join our true selves and visualize going down an inner path inside our body.

Perhaps it would help to "see" your spirit going past your vocal chords or your lungs, as it makes its way to your spark of centered grace and holiness. You know the spark is there. You can and will remember that place where you were and still are with God. From all eternity, before you were born, the spark of God was you, and God's need to love formed you.

"If you are not willing to risk the usual, you will have to settle for the ordinary." Jim Rohn

"All our dreams can come true if we have the courage to pursue them." Walt Disney

Let's spend time finding our center now. Stay where you are and be alone with the love of God that formed you.

Write about this meditational experience. How hard or easy was it to understand and implement?

What specific, natural or automatic, twists were you able to discover for yourself?

What does your energy spark of holy look like?

_____

_____

_____

_____

_____

_____

Take a moment to go back to Day 18's Poem 15 called "Our Test" and re-read the poem from your centering/depth perspective. Now we are expanding our journaling thoughts, or pausing. This meditation pausing is always an eye-opener for me. Writing is my way of emptying everything out so as to really allow me an opportunity to see what is going on in my life. God works within our efforts to reach the holy because God desires unity. Which of the last few poems found on Day 18 caused pause for you? What physical plane crisis or time of chaos has softened your own awareness of the passing NOW?

Continue your journal work for today.

More spiritual plane deep work:

With the deep searching and varied longings found in those poems of struggle for Day 18, use the next song, Anoint Me, Lord, to transform your stance and support your surrender to the openness of God's plans for you.

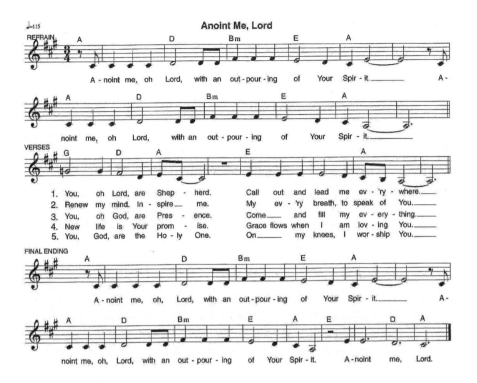

Anoint Me, Lord

REFRAIN

A - noint me, oh Lord, with an out - pour - ing of Your Spir - it._____ A -

noint me, oh Lord, with an out - pour - ing of Your Spir - it._____

VERSES

1. You, oh Lord, are Shep - herd. Call out and lead me ev - 'ry - where.____
2. Renew my mind. In - spire__ me. My ev - 'ry breath, to speak of You.____
3. You, oh God, are Pres - ence. Come__ and fill my ev - ery - thing.____
4. New life is Your prom - ise. Grace flows when I am lov - ing You.____
5. You, God, are the Ho - ly One. On__ my knees, I wor - ship You.____

FINAL ENDING

A - noint me, oh, Lord, with an out - pour - ing of Your Spir - it._____ A -

noint me, oh, Lord, with an out - pour - ing of Your Spir - it. A - noint me, Lord.

April 25, 2011 Words and Music by Patricia Jean Smithyman-Zito.

www.LivingInTheNowBook.com/music

Action Step: (Spiritual Plane)

Spend time comparing your place within the tone and perspectives of song 6, Anoint Me, Lord, to the previous song 5, on Day 18, Oh, God, Make Haste. This has been a true spiritual plane work day so stay deep for as long as you can!

Physical Plane Merger ~ Day 22 ~ Meditation

"Uncontrolled, the hunger and thirst after God may become an obstacle, cutting off the soul from what it desires. If a man would travel far along the mystic road, he must learn to desire God intensely but in stillness, passively and yet with all his heart and mind and strength." Aldous Huxley

When you are ready, find your quiet space and begin your meditation to go deeper into your true self again. Let's purposefully turn off all outside noises, listen, and come to love the surrounding silence. Notice how you quiet yourself. Again, let us really focus on our breathing and relax every muscle in our body. Filling our heart with happiness, peace and love, let's empty our mind of the day's pressures, concerns and commitments. Just for now, let's find our holy place deep within and choose to remain there. Let's invite God and allow God to anoint us with an outpouring of Spirit to guide our way. Pray the words of the song from yesterday, Day 21, Anoint Me, Lord – Song 6, and surrender to this holy time. Pray the words over and over to surrender more and to include the mental plane's fervor.

Let's try looking around this holy place within. Please take notice of things by creating them with your imagination. We can use the supports of our natural sense of thinking and doing things in the real world to explore this inner spirit world. It is everything we choose to make it!

Let's begin the inner journey to our holy space. Allow the needed amount of time to quiet the outside world around you. Use your spiritual tools to move within your being and rest in your space of holy. It is good to be here! You've been here before, remember?

Now let's journey into an experience in our inner world together. I want you to walk with me now. Let's travel, side by side, down this narrow path, past a meadow, through a flower patch, into a small cluster of trees, and out and then to an open backyard.

Look ahead. There is a house.

It's nobody's house, yet it is everyone's house. It is your house and my house.

Let's go inside.

Come with me to the east wing where there are hallways of rooms with closed doors.

Look at each door. There are labels on the doors.

Read them with me. *Sad ~ Happy ~ No ~ Yes ~ Good ~ Bad Crying ~ Laughing ~ Singing ~ Dancing ~ Screaming Doubting ~ Believing ~ Trusting ~ Weak ~ Strong ~ Joy Forgiving ~ Questioning ~ Understanding ~ Whispering*

What other labels do you see? There are so many more areas of need. Visualize the doors.

Think about these words and other labels you feel should be showing as choice rooms to enter.

Write them here.

Write about your inward journey today. Was it easy to do? Can you tell of what *you* saw?

Write your thoughts here too. Speak of your own details of the journey inward. The path offered to us today is the path of love, a path in which the initiative is always taken by God. God invites us to accept grace and to allow everlasting love to love us NOW. Gradually, we learn of surrender and then we see how to live constantly aware of

God's presence. Write with awareness of the spiritual plane running parallel to your physical and mental planes.

"I am in the process of making positive changes in all areas of my life." Louise Hays

_____

_____

_____

_____

_____

_____

_____

_____

_____

_____

_____

_____

_____

_____

_____

_____

_____

_____

_____

_____

_____

_____

_____

Action Step: (Physical Plane)

Spend some time mastering how you master your physical and mental planes while exploring the inner house we visited and choose to move about in your inner spiritual plane space. Fully harness the 3 planes of energy and bring them into your NOW.

Drink more water for this sit and sip time and give thanks for the well-being you are able to experience.

Extend Yourself ~ Day 23 ~ A Reach Through Planes

"The great thing about new friends is that they bring new energy to your soul." Shanna Rodriguez

Today is a perfect day to journey! Shall we go inside together? Okay, good, my friend!

Let's knock on the Sad door today. I prefer going there together, don't you? The least we can do is knock. Jesus says knock and it shall be opened unto you. I believe. You believe too.

Open the door that says Sad. Let's go through the door and sit in the chairs to be with that emotion, to recognize it, allow it and listen to it. It's okay to scream and cry, to pace the floor with fists raised. It's okay to be in the grocery store pushing your cart with tears streaming down your face. You can now own your sadness, label it, embrace it, and learn from it. You can put it aside then, walk out of the room, and close the door. Looking back, you can choose to go on.

Perhaps we will open the door to happiness or peace next. There sits our Lord and Savior, Jesus Christ! No walking into this room! Jesus is there, with a big smile of unconditional love on His face and His welcoming arms spread wide! Here is when we run, screaming, into the arms of our Beloved One! Here, Jesus enfolds us, fills us, and reminds us of love's power. It is in this room that we remember how we are meant to feel. Here, we can actually feel how precious we are.

Relief from the tedium and power struggles of day-to-day drudgeries fade from our attention in this room. Here is where we need to stay! It is as elemental as life itself that we work on the way we feel, transport the feelings to our thoughts, project them into our being through prayer, and believe in the always available abundance of grace and presence at our fingertips. Jesus, our Word made flesh, always surrounding us, always vibrating love's message of purpose, hope and joy. We need to remember how that feels and bring those feelings to the surface of our everyday world.

Yes, it is now, in this room with our Almighty, in this holy moment, that we realize how different the Sad room was. We understand that we still need to go into those rooms of trouble to be alone, to understand and feel everything in life, and to learn of purpose. Ah, but it is best in these rooms where God becomes joyfully present. Perhaps, in time, we will come to know ourselves well enough to notice God is present in those rooms of trouble too. So let's stay in the arms of the Word made flesh for just a bit longer. I don't want to part from presence just yet, do you? Feel Jesus holding you. Look at yourself sitting with Him. Listen to His words. Allow Jesus to fill you again and remember how you are feeling (using the mental plane skills) so you can bring that abundance back to the physical plane world when you leave this spiritual plane world.

"Each day God imprints on us and within us a touch of the infinite, a longing for life, a yearning for unending love; we know Him as hidden and distant yet visible and near. He calls us from one degree of awareness to another, from one sense of being possessed to another realization of it." Fr. Edward J. Farrell

Express your words of feeling the feelings and thinking the thoughts to move through the planes.

Tell Jesus anything, everything, something, nothing.

Going deeper into the connections within our mental plane: We are finding ways to connect. Kything is another way of connecting—being spiritually present to another. Kything is coming to understand how we can speak and listen with our heart and communicate by being still. Kything is speaking soul to soul. Kything is an old English word meaning to come to a person without a mask, plain, as you are. To kythe means to come to another as you are.

It was wonderful resting in the arms of Jesus in our happy room today.

Realize, too, that there are angels present, adoring Jesus with you. Kything is very real, and oftentimes, it takes traumas of death or deep sadness to empty us and force us to know what the busy world does not want to know.

Action Step: (Mental Plane)

So come and journey within. Choose to be silent, still, and poised. Choose life. Choose to become more. Choose to be happy. Become a companion on the journey!

We are many! We are KYTHING!

The next poem is one I like to type out and give, with a handkerchief, to anyone who is going through the death of a loved one. It is my hope and my prayer that they are able to step into the spiritual world while they are being forced to stop and look at the fragilities and limitations of the physical world. Feel free to use this poem, changing a word or two, to meet your needs and the needs of the receiver, if you wish. Just fold the poem into a handkerchief and suggest they keep it with them during their hard times and then use it to wipe away the tears of times ahead. I believe it can help them connect with their loved one because of the prayer power of the giver, the depth of loss for the receiver, and the love, now in spirit form, of the deceased. They cannot come back to the physical plane, but we can most certainly move into the spiritual plane.

Assure them of your prayers and your loving thoughts, which will support their days of discovering the spiritual plane world after everything is over and life's realities settle in for them.

This Handkerchief ~ Poem 20

Please accept this handkerchief from me.
This simple cloth has Kything powers, you see.
As gift, it is given to capture all your tears,
Softening them to prayer down through the years.

You must hold it to your lips when times are bad.
Wipe away your tears when life seems much too sad.
Treasure and keep safe this cloth these days
To carry what you must with love and praise.

There are a million prayers contained within.
They all become alive when this cloth touches skin.
So keep it with you always as you trod
To connect with your beloved, united now with God.

I share this handkerchief meditation with you because I have found it to be a powerful and personal way to be truly present to and truly present with someone who must give a loved one back to God. Consider these next words as a suggestion or thought starter for your own card ideas.

> Please accept my deepest sympathy, and still, thoughts of celebrations combine, for we know that your beloved is dancing with Jesus and celebrating life's journey. I know you will miss your beloved. Wonderful people blast into our hearts, our minds, and our lives and leave a hole where once we were whole with them. Hold and use this handkerchief as a way of connecting, across the physical plane, to your loved one, and find peace in your times of prayer and quiet listening. You will know presence and share joy by being immersed in love at the spiritual level. My prayers will continue to support you as you reflect on everything in your NOW.

The handkerchief can be the medium to use to help us grasp the process of learning more about the journey of the soul. We have to understand the need to create the self-talk necessary to journey through this physical world, making sense of death and confirming everlasting life. The handkerchief idea is one way to help us become more connected. Again, death, suffering, pain, disappointment, and loss are all part of the physical plane world, and most try to avoid confrontation with such issues. By spending time in the spiritual plane world, we are able to look at any moment of living life to the fullest as God's time. It is not good or bad, right or wrong, happy or sad. It is God moving me closer to my own truth and helping me to understand myself and my journey better. Jesus tells us that it is with faith that all things are possible. We learn to know about our gift of faith by spending time in the holy, in our spiritual plane. Within grace, we are able to sing our song in every moment.

Everybody has a special song. Nobody can sing anybody else's song for them. You cannot sing my song, and I cannot sing your song. As companions on the journey, we can sing in harmony, double our praise, and fill others and our world with grace.

Yes, as companions on the journey, we can sing in harmony, double our praise, and fill others and our world with grace.

This next reflection is a song. One of my favorites! Everybody has a special song to sing.

In this song, it says, "First time I met you, I just knew I'd have to sing along."

I have met you. I know you because of your loss, pain, grieving, fear and human needs. I recognize your smile and that twinkle in your eye, your sure step, your strong hand and your wise words. We are all the same. Don't let the outside world fool you. The journey is the journey for everyone. Some people appear to have all the answers and appear happy, focused, driven. They may have a spiritual journey that provides answers for them, or they may have a few good masks to wear so nobody touches them. They, too, have a special song.

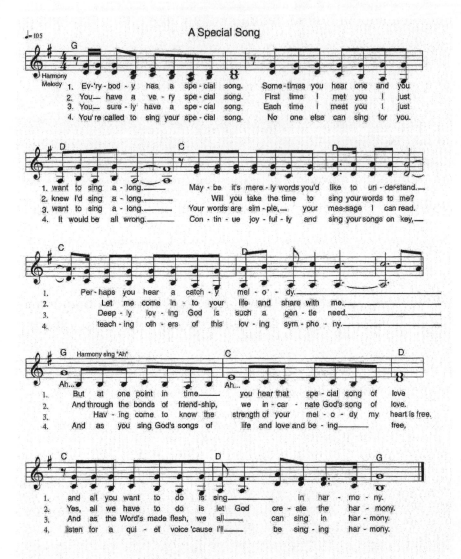

December 5, 1983 Words and Music by Patricia Jean Smithyman-Zito.

www.LivingInTheNowBook.com/music

The truth is, we are called to be companions on the journey in the physical plane and to walk with our Incarnate Word, learning to say our unconditional yes to loving. Once we grasp the concepts of this physical plane, we can work more deeply on the mental plane and discover a greater awareness of the spiritual plane. For now, please ponder the points of my song and know that I am singing this to y-o-u.

What are the words in your special song?

How able are you to live each moment with grace, knowing God is working all for good?

Who sings harmony for your song? Can you hear my harmony too?

Do you know how to bridge the gap from the physical world into the spiritual world?

_____

_____

_____

_____

_____

_____

_____

_____

Action Step: (Spiritual Plane)

Explain the awareness of your soul's journey NOW.
Explain the awareness of your soul's NOW journey.

God is the name we dare to speak to name the One we worship. The Bible tells us story after story of faithful followers and not-so-faithful followers. Within these stories, we develop an understanding of God, and our religious traditions give us a foundation upon which to connect with the Holy One and to better understand our relationship with the Holy One.

Existing before the beginning of everything, God simply is. God is forever. God is the Alpha and the Omega. God is the beginning and the end. Jesus, God's Word, became a human being to help us better understand the breadth, depth, and height of God's abundant love. God does everything to lead us to love and union. God is God: good and gracious. Over all and in all, God is listening and guiding, loving and forgiving.

We Come before You for More ~ Poem 21

We stand alone between two worlds, and we cannot seem to focus.
We can touch the fringy edges of Your presence,
but how do we gather substance?

Can You temper this whole-body-spirit-person of rough edges?
Can You spill Your love into this valley where we stand?

Oh, that You fill our worlds to the very brim
with enough love to overflow meaning.

All else pales to eternity with You.

We are no place at all, yet it is everywhere that we may unhinge You.
Oh, simplify our efforts to be,
expose our dualistic thinking,
soften our hardened hearts,

renew our faith,
for we long to gaze upon Your face in both worlds.

Lift the veil from our flat dreams of the valley.
Transform us and take us to the mountain peaks and beyond.

Be with us in this endless search for more that our true good,
Our holy, can unfold within Incarnate Love.

> Wisdom has built her house, she has set up seven columns; she has dressed her meat, mixed her wine, yes she has spread her table. She has sent out her maidens, she calls from the heights out over the city; "Let whoever is simple turn in here. To the one who lacks understanding, she says, "Come eat of my food, and drink of the wine I have mixed! Forsake foolishness that you may live; advance in the way of understanding." (Proverbs 9:1–6)

I have confessed that I have not always been wise. I know my interpretations of wisdom, truth and love have often been subjectively convenient. Paths chosen and choices made, from personally created realities, are what I call hell. In God's created realities, everything speaks the truth, is good, and leads me to a better understanding of who I am in God. Only then am I happy, free, growing, and truly living this journey of abundant awareness, and I call that heaven. Heaven is being united with God's everything. So, yes, heaven starts here!

I want this body to be transformed, and that happens through consciousness of God's energy (presence) in my being, my world, my NOW. To have such a vision of wisdom, I must know the importance of an external focus (God) in my thoughts, prayers, meditations, words and actions. Such experiences of awareness, illumination, and grace pour out in music, musings, poems, art, and grateful, righteous, holy, abundant living. The external manifestations are expressions of my internal life with the awareness of God.

This physical plane can be transformed by our inwardly directed experience of spiritual presence, which shatters all limits. Even with just a mere second or two of such mystical presence, we can expand our need for God and change our limited visions of truth, love and happiness.

Submission, surrender, and openness of our mind, heart, and will allows wisdom to grace us with an understanding of our inner world, divine presence, and reality's truth.

That is the tension creating the balance. Creating space for prayer is removing myself from the physical plane, from sensory involvement, and there, I can find my "spark" of God within, that inward focus of my spiritual plane. Turning away from the physical plane (the world's misconceptions, alienations, and everyday busyness) and turning toward God (our spiritual plane awareness of happiness and peace) is what I call holiness.

I desire to be holy. I desire to be holier. Do you understand? What does it mean to be holy? What does it mean to be full of God? Do you desire more depth, more happiness, more prayer, more purpose, more presence in your journey? I long to be wise.

One day at a time. One step, one word; one awareness of choosing happiness, union, presence; and one more moment of letting go of self.

One more *yes* to the known, the unknown, the easy to accept, and the not so easy to accept.

Forever In You

REFRAIN

In wis-dom and char-i-ty You brought us to life. In mer-cy and grace You sent Your Son. Now Your love must cause us to die as we learn to live for-ev-er in You.

VERSES

Harmony
Melody

1. Give us the wa-ter of new birth. Give us pres-ence and Eu-cha-rist, lov-ing, as peo-ple of God. Refrain

2. Help us to glo-ri-fy our God. Help us to im-i-tate the Son. Grow-ing in the grace of Spir-it. Refrain

3. Grant us sta-bil-i-ty of heart. Grant us firm-ness of will, liv-ing a pur-pose filled life. Refrain

June 5, 2010 Words and Music by Patricia Jean Smithyman-Zito.

www.LivingInTheNowBook.com/music

I desire to be holy. I desire to be holier. The journey shows me that I struggle with that a lot. It's not easy to surrender. It is not easy to be happy. We all make mistakes. It's about the journey, the becoming more, the coming to know self and know God. Ponder the words of the song "Forever in You" again and then wander through a few poems of when things are not as we would like them to be. We are all there a lot of the time. The truth is the truth. We are human, and we struggle, we fall, we give up hope, and we give less than is expected of us, seeing ego and selfishness permeate and distort our truth. Admitting to who we are, in our own truth, is a conquering of the mental plane. Honesty, to others and to self, is the best policy and the hardest concept to master because ego simply won't allow it. Then again, it is in the struggling that we learn to lean on our inner strength and trust in Almighty's grace and mercy.

"Things work out best for those who make the best of how things work out." John Wooden

Comments can be written here or kept in your heart of hearts.

Who are you really? Not what you do for a living. Not where you live. Not what you've accomplished thus far in your journey. Who are y-o-u? What is it that prevents you from being what your heart, mind and soul desire you to be?

Going deeper:

God's Gift Is Today ~ Poem 22

Carrying secrets over the years
will create a life of confusion and tears.

Most of my life, I've lived two lives,
either driven by fear or paralyzed.

I was never quite sure who I was inside,
innocence stolen, person denied.

But by living so no one would ever see,
contradictions and conflicts overpowered me.

Don't let shame and guilt and hate preside.
Please don't keep it all inside.

Let things go, realizing it is okay.
Live in each moment for God's gift is today.

Remember that you can listen to the song as you read the words. Go to the link shown at the end of each song sheet.
www.LivingInTheNowBook.com/music

Come, Lord

July 2, 2012 Words and Music by Patricia Jean Smithyman-Zito.
www.LivingInTheNowBook.com/music

The Form of Jesus ~ Poem 23

I've always wanted what was good and right,
But nothing could fill that need.
I decided I was too tired to fight.
Told God how I long to be freed.

Feeling bad or guilty or even abused,
I deserve to suffer and die.
I'll never get back times I haven't used.
"Go away, God, I'm too tired to try."

Shattered with every instant replay,
I bear the guilt, the shame, the lies.
What is the price I have to pay?
God said, "No more compromise."

So we gathered up all my past one day.
I helped God nail it to a tree.
It took the form of Jesus as I walked away,
Redemption humbles me.

Action Step: (Physical Plane)

Write about how we can admit who we are to find our own truth.

What external work have you come to rely on since beginning our journey together?

Still spending time in precise, critical thinking, let's continue the journey of facing the truth to manifest God's greatest visions of the true me and the true you. More deep work today!

After Brokenness ~ Poem 24

Codependent no more, I stand on the shore of a tumultuous history.
To conquer each weakness, in God-centered meekness,
is a purification, you see.

Increasing cognition, through total submission,
will finally set my heart free. Healing a past,
put together at last, there is hope in all that will be.

I let go of controls and living out roles and all kinds of insanity.
I'll face what is real and believe what I feel.
After brokenness comes victory.

This letting go is so hard for me. I think I've faced ego's lies of fear, guilt, shame, pride and depression a thousand times over. And I'm still walking on that edge, teetering between both worlds, praying for strength, purpose, and wisdom to see the frailty of this physical plane.

> God will strengthen you, so that you will be blameless
> on the day of our Lord Jesus Christ. God is faithful
> and it was God who called you to fellowship with the
> Son, Jesus Christ our Lord. (1 Corinthians 1:8–9)

Am I ever going to be strong, believing beyond feelings and fears, admitting the moments of blatant selfishness and the obvious vacillating of unresolved hope? Will I constantly struggle to conquer the truth of my mental plane?

There is no limit to love's forbearance, to its trust,
its hope, its power to endure. Love never fails.
(1 Corinthians 13:7–8)

"Motivation gets you going and habit gets you there. Make motivation
a habit and you will get there more quickly and have more fun on the
trip." Zig Ziglar

In the discovery process of maturing into the true me, I am creating
habits on the physical plane to make my life easier and to make my
body healthier. Motivation is triggered in my mind, and it is when I
face the truth of what I say versus what I do, that I find strength in
my vision of God's abundance and unconditional love. God sees me
as my true best self. When I meet the true me on the mental plane, I
am holy. It is a constant struggle to master the physical plane and an
even more demanding challenge to quiet the mental plane.

The Chimes in My Heart ~ Poem 25

I cannot hear the mystic music
that God's inexplicable presence reveals.
The pomp and circumstance of living becomes an unsurfaced control.

I function with ascending and descending feelings,
unaware of how outside influences mute my melodies.
Without the subtlest sign, strangers participate in my life.

How have I allowed them to stifle my song?
God's breezes are not stilled.
Is it somehow that I am too filled with fears and feelings inside to
chime anymore?
Am I holding on so tightly that I can no longer sway to God's
invitational score?

I have become weary being tossed about in storms.

To chime beautifully, in the midst of compulsory thinking,
only allows the outside listener pleasure.
What about me?

I just feel battered about and too tired to try.

In the center of all turbulence is peace.
Take me to my center, to the chimes in my heart.
I need to hear again the musical raptures God shares that heighten
the treasured rhythms.

The chimes of happiness, the treasured rhythms of being free, that
mystical music of my spiritual world can and does change the way
I live.
I want to be happy. I want to love.
I surely struggle but I am listening.

Habits can be put into practice on the physical plane to support my
efforts to tap into my full potential right NOW.
Course corrections that should be strong habits by now are:
Plan my day the night before.
Start eliminating poor behaviors.
Be intentional about living my truth.
Always speak kindly and always speak the truth.
Deepen relationships with respectful words and actions.
Make wellness a priority.
Have specific Sit-and-Sip times in the structure of my morning,
afternoon and evening.
Name my blessings.
Use my gifts and talents to serve.
Spend time in prayer to become more human because there is how I
become more divine.

Continuing our deep work:

Childhood Weaknesses ~ Poem 26

To repair my childhood weaknesses,
There are new behaviors I must learn. I must
actively find help and see being healthy as my main concern.

Options taken during childhood,
which may have helped me stay alive,
were often necessary evils then, motivations to survive.

But without consistent parenting
throughout each important stage, I find
developmental holes in mastering certain growth tasks for each age.

It is a never-ending process
to understand and know each feeling. But as I
repair my childhood weaknesses, I find friendship fosters healing.

So face the truth in everything.
Feel the grieving and the pain.
Regret what wasn't given to you. Rejoice in growing up again.

We are all in this together. Companions on the journey can share
God's greatest vision in the hunger and thirst to be more in God's
image and likeness, NOW. Making God's love our own is the first
step to holiness. Jesus showed us that to become fully human we
must use our gifts and help each other. We need to know this NOW
because the secret to making each day our best day unfolds in our
becoming holy and being a servant.

Oh, Excuse Me

♩=140

Guitar Capo 2

REFRAIN 1

Oh, ex - cuse me, I've got to have a word with You!

Oh, ex - cuse me. I'd like to speak to You.

1. Lord, we're try - ing hard to serve You.____ Each new day has a

chal - lenge of its own. How can we be sure we know the way?

How can we say that we'll nev - er walk a - lone?____ (Refrain 1)

2. Sis - ters, we must con - tin - ue to serve God.____ Each new day has a

chal - lenge of its own. Will you help me to know the way?____

We must work to make God's love our own.____ (To Refrain 2)

REFRAIN 2

Oh, ex - cuse me. I've got to have a word with You.

August 24, 1969 Words and Music by Patricia Jean Smithyman-Zito.

www.LivingInTheNowBook.com/music

NOW Moments - Real Moments ~ Poem 27

Time is passing constantly
Yet, our real moments are too few.
The minutes become hours, days,
Months, then years of things to do.

Things to do take up our days
And suddenly life is spent.
We've hardly stopped at all, it seems,
To enjoy "NOW's" main event.

How do you see your life, my friend,
From what I've shared with you?
Does your world evolve in black and white,
Or is it filled with colors, too?

Black and white surely have their place,
So I speak of all that's real.
But life requires love as well,
NOW moments we must learn to feel.

So let's put down our everything,
To visit, laugh and play.
Let's let real moments fill our lives,
For love is all we need today.

A thought for course correction:

"You'll never change your life until you change something you do daily. The secret of your success is found in your daily routine."
John C. Maxwell

"Good habits formed at youth make all the difference." Aristotle

"Chains of habit are too light to be felt until they are too heavy to be broken." **Warren Buffet**

Blend together our opening conversation, the poems and the songs. Personally ponder your hunger and thirst within God's image and vision of y-o-u and how this mental plane mastery can bring you to becoming aware of being holy in your NOW.

_____

_____

_____

_____

_____

_____

_____

_____

_____

_____

_____

_____

_____

Action Step: (Mental Plane)

Write out your physical plane and mental plane course corrections found within your deep work today. What is it you want to target from our prayer time today?

Facing my true self is critical. Knowing I am not doing it alone is my salvation.

Look to Your Angel ~ Poem 28

Kythe to me, call me, explain all your fear.
Tell me your truth, for I promise to hear.

I am within you. Touch the star in your heart.
Just look to your angel when falling apart.

Yes, you have an angel, a spiritual friend,
Who stands close beside you with love that won't end.

Do you have a real, live, personal angel who helps mirror your true self?

Are you an angel to others? Our true self is only discovered within relationship.

Are you blessed to have a friend, soul-mate, lover, spouse or family member to be your companion on the journey?

I Belong To You

1. I— be-long to you. You— be-long to me.— I pledge you all my love, my dear, I al-ways will be true._For ev - er - since I've met you,— my life has been ful - filled. I've found such hap - pi - ness in be - com - ing part of you.—

2. You be-long to me. I— be-long to you.— You've pro-mised me your love, my dear, you al-ways will be true. Why is it you can love me so? How is it love can grow? You've found your love ful- filled in be - com-ing part of me.— We

3. find new life in Christ. He gives—— new life to us.— Our cov - e - nant of love we seal. We vow our lives to

You, Pro-tect and guide our new love and bless our - u - nit - y. We
found our love ful - filled in be - com- ing part of You.
4. I give life for you. You give life for Me. I know how much you
love, My friends, you've built your love on Me. Be warm and un - der - stand - ing.
Trea-sure each oth-er's love. And now go out in peace, My peace I give to
you. To you, My peace I leave with you.

November 18, 1972 Words and Music by Patricia Jean Smithyman-Zito.

www.LivingInTheNowBook.com/music

<u>My True Friend! ~ Poem 29</u>

Every day she makes her way down the streets of endless giving.
Life's not that easy for her, but being a woman,
she is compelled by years of inner emotions
and past experiences of trying to love intensely.
No one really notices her absorbing drivenness.
That's because she's calm, cool, collected; focused.

Everyone assumes she is going and doing all the
responsible things she's always done.
You'd never know, just to look at her, of all she does.
Everyone looks to her too.
She's impressive, knowledgeable; quality.

She is in the fore, yet in the background, loving, leading, praying.
I bet people figure she is just about perfect.
You'd think so too if you met her.
I dare you to speak to her, be present to the holy she treasures,
feel the amatory air and mischievousness she hoards.

I love the chance to be with her. She's my other self.
Very busy all the time, but happy in her heart.
I tell her how I worry and of things for which I pray.
I don't think you could not once you meet her.
She is so amicable, unique, wise; treasured.

I admire her. I'm probably jealous too, for I need her so.
I pray for her every day.
I respect her. I really love her.
I treasure my companion on the journey,
my friend, my sister, my buddy, my pal
who knows my truth and loves me unconditionally.
I hope you have a true friend too.

"Motivation is the fuel necessary to keep the human engine running."
Zig Ziglar

How do you feel after spending serious time with yourself?

Do you find yourself expand eternally when you include your angel,
your significant other, your friends, your God?

_____

_____

_____

_____

_____

_____

_____

_____

_____

_____

_____

_____

_____

_____

_____

_____

_____

_____

_____

_____

_____

_____

_____

_____

Action Step: (Spiritual Plane)

Talk about your relationship with the significant others in your life. The circle of love unfolds and establishes our safety-net to become fully alive within the expansion.

My Spirit's With You

February 11, 1976 Words and Music by Patricia Jean Smithyman-Zito.

www.LivingInTheNowBook.com/music

Let's take a break from the deep self-thinking for a moment and look at why we are who we are and why we do some of the things that we do from another perspective.

As a reading intervention specialist during much of my teaching career, I worked with a lot of young people who did not find much success in the "normal" classroom setting. Oftentimes, this learning struggle left them with poor self-esteem and a lack of understanding as to how they could succeed in the classroom or in their life. I would take two specific approaches or present two suggestions to them whenever they would join my classes. First, we would try to come to an understanding of the ways that the brain works. Secondly, we would look at ways to eliminate distractions and false truths, which can inhibit everyone's success.

I want to get into a bit of that way of thinking through things now. I believe it enables us all to better grasp the how, the why, and the ways we judge ourselves. I mentioned earlier that I was very unaware of my life, my world, or my spirituality during my younger years. Success in school was not something I was blessed to understand or enjoy. My mother and I put my books and my school uniforms in a big pile in the middle of the street and burned them after I graduated from high school, holding hands and singing joyfully, "We made it! We made it!"

Again, I simply didn't "get it" and didn't live in much awareness of my holy, abundant NOW. It wasn't until I went away to study sign language, in my late twenties, that I discovered I really had a brain that worked. Pretty sad, actually, but I didn't see myself as smart.

The dominant side of the brain in right-handed people is the left hemisphere, and it better processes language and linear, factual thinking. The dominant side of the brain in left-handed people is the right hemisphere, and it is filled with images and holistic ideas.

My grandmother and my mother shared that left-handed trait. I write right-handed but actually do most other things as a leftie, as does my mother. Right-handed people are usually dominant left-hemisphere people who tend to process facts, live on a schedule, and see details in things. It is the left-brained individual who finds success in most normal classroom settings, which tend to begin with details and move to the whole, bigger picture. The dominant right-hemisphere people (often lefties) tend to see things better as a whole rather than in parts and are usually not interested in details. They prefer getting to the point or to the end first and then look into how the details apply later.

I found personal satisfaction with signing, with music, with writing poetry, etc. because the right brain is the source of intuition and inspiration. I was always "out there, dreaming up something" instead of studying and giving back correct answers in school. Understanding how my right brain processes information helps me with every aspect of living. I now know how to arrange things for me to better find success. That is what I tried to teach my struggling students to understand. Looking at your brain's strengths, those intuitive gifts, and your natural abilities enables you to better structure what you are attempting to accomplish.

Relationships with true companions on the journey, interactions with others, being involved in people's lives, in social or religious causes, not only keeps you alive but also makes you real. Taking the initiative to find out what is going on in other people's lives and being involved in what is happening in our families, our neighborhoods, our churches, our schools, our government, and our world are our foundations, our becoming more, and our ways of knowing who we are through the eyes of others.

I pray for those I love and for our hurting world. It is important to be involved in life too for expansion, understanding, and awareness of self. Do you have people in your heart whom you've lost touch with? Are there significant others who have helped shape who you are? Who have you loved into becoming more? Do you miss them? Do they miss you? Perhaps communication with persons of impact will happen while you are reading and writing on our journey together. It's all good! It all needs to be right and that happens when we move beyond self to include every person, every situation and absolutely everything that our loving God has created for good.

Hello, Friend, Hello ~ Poem 30

Bridge distance between us with a familiar hello.
For my heart truly aches and I'm missing you so.

I need some security time with you.
There is nothing else I would rather do.

Come sit with me, our thoughts we can share.
I love you, my friend, and I genuinely care.

So relate your burdens and release your fear.
See your true self through our friendship mirror.

I, too, will envisage your guardianship,
As I sit by your side on our friendship trip.

As my response to you helps to brighten my day,
I will cogitate presence and quietly pray.

Oh, thank you, dear Lord, for my special friend,
Through whom the aches of the heart can mutually end.

How do you learn things?
What is your preferred style of learning? Do you like to listen, read, take notes or make things?

What are your natural strengths, abilities, tendencies? Is your right brain or your left brain more dominant, or are you balanced and use a little of both sides of your brain?

What are your gifts, and how have you used them to better your life, the lives of those you love, and our world?

When have you seen your true self through the eyes of another?

Who is it you should probably connect with?

Without regrets, where do we start to begin again?

_____

_____

_____

_____

_____

_____

_____

_____

_____

_____

_____

_____

_____

_____

_____

_____

_____

_____

_____

_____

_____

_____

Action Step: (Physical Plane)

How do we give grace to others?

My own personal action step for today is to thank Fr. Kevin Liebhardt, Fr. Lou Pizmoht and the many LIVING IN THE NOW members of St. Justin Martyr Parish with whom I prayed, celebrated and became a better person with for over 35 years of ministry together.

Forgiveness ~ Day 29 ~ Immeasurable Love

Beginning again is often forced upon us when we are too busy being busy. Traditionally, at the beginning of another year, we admit the obvious chaos and unproductive areas of our lives and create our New Year's resolutions to pacify our left brain's need for more efficiency and productivity, among other things. Thinking about what we'd like to accomplish for the coming year or establishing a list of personal goals that we feel can make us better people is beneficial for growth and essential for change.

It's also a bit overwhelming!

Basic things on the average person's "change list" include losing weight, eating better, getting more sleep, spending more time in prayer, stopping smoking, cutting back on drinking, earning more money, putting that clothes closet back together, enjoying time with family and friends, working less, exercising more, and putting an end to endless procrastinations. Issues of life in the physical plane demand our attention, our effectiveness, and our need to accomplish. I am a strong proponent of all those above changes! I also want to be happy.

If I continue doing the things I am doing, I will continue having the same results. Yes, starting over is a great idea. Changing is about admitting what isn't working and what is no longer a benefit to me and my world and acknowledging that if I stopped doing half the things I am doing, the world will continue on without me and be just fine!

After more than forty years of ministry, I have conceded that my focus on living life to the fullest is in the need to change stage again. I have been very involved in my faith since my early years of being a Religious Sister of the Incarnate Word in Cleveland, Ohio. The passion to making everyone's world brighter and more meaningful by exposing them to Incarnation and to the Word of God, bursting forth in their world as had happened in my world, energized me. I have followed my heart since that profound profession day of my final vows, made in 1974, of saying yes to God's invitation to love. I have been immersed in church as a pastoral associate, youth minister, member of parish council, member of the parish executive board, interpreter for the hearing impaired, and remedial math and reading teacher in many schools. I have been involved in the Music Ministry, the Parish School of Religion, the Special Education Ministry and the Parish Festival Committee. I have taught sign language classes and worked with fire and police forces in our local areas. I've also tried, with all my heart, to be the perfect and only daughter, an awesome sister to three brothers, an aunt, a cousin, a wife, a mother, a stepmom, and the absolute best grandmother on this earth.

Trying to make sense of the world, why things happen as they do, and believing that God works all for good leave me open to listening to my heart of hearts. I know nothing happens without God's plan for me unfolding. I am weak. I have made mistakes. I may still have profound regrets. I am also inclined to find a reason for everything that happens in life to be of purpose. I cannot fool myself of anything life-changing when I turn to my significant others and ask them to participate in my path of fulfillment. Love isn't to be shrugged off. Happiness is mine to take. My irrational thinking cannot be justified in my "rest of my life" truth. I need my friends and loved ones to know who I really am and enable shared happiness to surface.

> Again I tell you, if two of you join your voices on earth to pray for anything whatever, it shall be granted you by My Father in heaven. Where two or three are gathered in My name, there am I in their midst. (Matthew 18:19–20)

Have you watched the movie "Pollyanna" yet? Worth your time to see true perspective!

Whatever you believe, with conviction, becomes your reality.

I Hope It's Not Too Late ~ Poem 31

The yesterdays of my present moments
have made me feel a little ill.

But the tomorrows of my future moments
have made time stand still.

It's not really an issue of fear or pain
or the unresolved "to be."

But it's the energy of living all over again
that seems to drain the life out of me.

In the stillness of my present mind,
I try to spend time in NOW's quiet.

Though past and future, I still find,
haven't muted all their cries yet.

Slowly rebuilding my inner state,
I grow so impatient to grow.

I only hope that it's not too late
to live and love all I long to know.

Looking at choices made during my life should provide insight and
wisdom, but never regrets.

Choices should be seen as just that: choices. Not bad choices or
not good choices. God works with us in all choices and invites us
to wonder and grace in this abundant NOW. We easily become
judgmental, self-critical, often agonizing about how differently
we'd live if we could just make those choices over again. Often, we

remain victims of regret, missing opportunities set before us to learn, grow, and contribute to the moment we are in. Nothing happens by accident. For every cause, there is an effect and everything happens as it should, working out for good.

There is a time and place for questioning regrets though. In formation of one's life, moments of decision-making, asking if I will have regrets if I choose this or that, is paramount. I used to tell my children to ask themselves an important question before deciding to do anything: What will happen if I do this? They began asking important questions as toddlers: What will happen if I play in the street? What will happen if I jump in the water without Mom watching? What will happen in the morning if I stay up too late at night? What will happen if I drive too fast?

In every moment of decision-making, be it large or small, asking if I will have regrets if I choose this option is a sign of becoming more mature. In the first stages of our lives, we only have two choices in every decision: right or wrong, good or bad, happy or sad, healthy or unhealthy, selfish or unselfish, holy or unholy, etc. Learning of life and love can be likened to holding up two fingers and literally asking behavior-based questions of either-or and then moving forward with the well-identified, better choice. This growth stage should happen early in one's discoveries of the *others* in their life and lead to the understanding that *others* are just as important as *I* am in the making of decisions.

Greater purpose, deeper Spirit-living, genuine happiness, and empowering self-control are life-changing results of authentic living in the NOW and are the blessings of wisdom and grace. I stand before myself in the mirror, (physical plane) and accept the beauty of God within (mental plane), forgiving, learning, and becoming more in the NOW (spiritual plane.)

I'm Walking with Me ~ Poem 32

The truth of my life
bring tears to my eyes.

The feelings I'm facing
should not be a surprise.

Somehow, I've buried experiences so deep,
because of the heartache I thought I must keep.

But now I am facing my own disbelief.
I'm feeling the pain, and I'm sharing the grief.

To let go of the ache, the anger, the shame
will give me the life I want to acclaim.

The growth that takes place in my little child's heart
will give me the power to finally start

living the way I believe I should be.
It has to be better now. I'm walking with me.

What choices from the past torment you? How can you make peace
with yourself and break free from past events? How has your childhood
managed to undermine abilities to believe in life's abundance?

Can you permit God and yourself to heal the wounds but still leave
the scars so perspectives of wisdom and grace can be realized?

Wounds hurt. Scars rarely have pain. If I have a memory and still
wince, I need to ask what I must do to forgive the issue within myself
and go to God with the burden. The witness of my life (my physical
plane) readies me to be wholeheartedly transformed (my mental
plane) into a deeper union with God and others (my spiritual plane.)

_____

_____

_____

_____

_____

_____

_____

_____

_____

_____

_____

Action Step: (Mental Plane)

There is a presence of God which can only be experienced in silence and solitude.

Spend time in prayer and, when you are ready, let's end today with the song Heal Me.

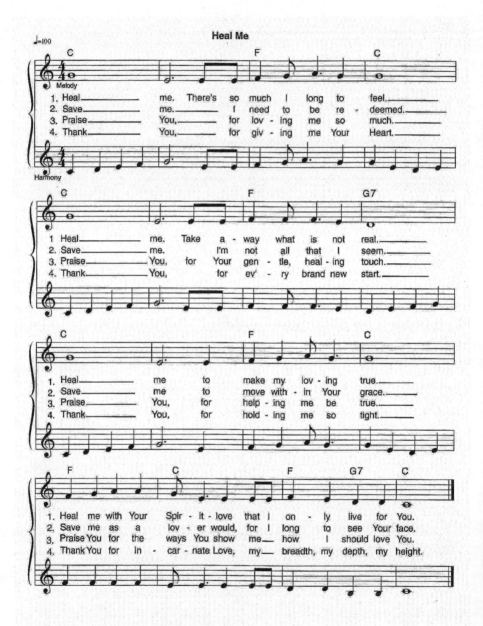

Heal Me

May 28, 2003 Words and Music by Patricia Jean Smithyman-Zito.

www.LivingInTheNowBook.com/music

Biggest Influencers ~ Day 30 ~ All Choice

We have rules and laws to keep us safe and productive. Eventually, within wisdom, grace and depth of vision, we come to live beyond the boundaries and structures we've once needed to live well. In our personal maturity, we do what is right with little or no regard to laws or rules.

Looking at myself, while in my NOW, is an inward experience. I am always standing off to the side, watching myself—not so much to be critical but more so to be purposefully aware of being genuine, attentive, positive and happy.

I really try to replace blame, guilt, helplessness, and regret with awareness of personal choice and positive powers of control. Being an eternal optimist who sees each moment as an abundant gift is not easy to do!

Let's expect more, plan for more, making a conscious effort to enjoy life's moments more by being present, aware and grateful! Embracing life's moments as an active participant is so much better than the limited boundaries of should or should-not and will leave us regretting nothing.

I believe this to be the beginning of awareness of the mental plane. This is fully realized after we leave the physical plane and the limitations of trying to be real. In the mental plane, all we see is who we really are/or were. There is no pretense, no more lies, no more ego, or no more false truths. The need on the mental plane is simply to see myself in truth and speak in truth. Perhaps this is the Roman Catholic Church's place after death called purgatory! Remember purgatory? That is the place or state following death in which penitent souls are purified of their venial sins or undergo the temporal punishment still remaining for forgiven mortal sins. Only after time in purgatory is the soul ready for heaven. I refer to this phase of our journey as the mental plane, and I believe the "punishment" or "suffering" we must work through, during this part of the journey, is to know the truth about how we lived out the gift of life.

We know what God knows then and admit to who we are. I cannot look into love's presence until I am truly all God has asked of me to become. I cannot be with truth until I know, accept, and love my own truth. Salvation promised. I seek God's presence, which has always sought me. There lies the happiness because I now control my NOW and trust my power to choose within the physical and mental planes.

That leads me to the spiritual plane, and it is a choice I have prepared for during my journey in the physical and mental planes. Honestly striving to choose presence during life in the physical plane and being true to myself in the mental plane enables me to choose presence for all eternity in the spiritual plane. God waits for our choosing and unconditionally welcomes us back. God wants us to choose.

> When the Paraclete comes, the Spirit of Truth, who comes from the Father and whom I (Jesus) Myself will send from the Father, God, Father, will bear witness on My behalf. You must bear witness as well, for you have been with Me from the beginning.
> (John 16:26–27)

We must heal our wounded hearts; correct what it is we long for; understand we are on a journey of happiness, peace, and love; and allow ourselves to move within God's abundant grace in this NOW. Our lover awaits our fulfillment of the plan from all eternity.

We are our own biggest influencer. How we act and what we think enables us to remain empty or become completely filled with grace, NOW.

Continuing to go deeper: We believe what our mind tells us.

I was walking down this dark alley one evening and heard someone cough. There must be danger lurking by this dumpster, I thought! Being quite taken aback by another's sounds, I instantly felt my heart racing, my legs becoming like rubber, and my breathing becoming shallow. There was nothing I could do to make my body even move. There was nothing I could think to change my body's responses to my first thoughts.

Just a story, but very true! Suppose I was walking down that same dark alley one evening, expecting to meet my daughter at the bend ahead. Hearing someone cough would have a totally different meaning for me and illicit a totally different bodily response. Ah, she is already waiting for me, I think! Being anxious to meet up with her, my step would lighten, my body would be filled with all the love I have for her, and I would break into a huge smile as I walked closer to the sounds. There would be no racing heart or breaking into a sweat from what I was thinking.

We subconsciously believe what our mind tells us. Truth is, we believe most of what the world tells us too. If you want to believe your life is lonely or that you never get the breaks you deserve, then that is what you will find in your universe. I want to believe I can live as Jesus lived, creating love, hope, peace and real miracles!

Look at this use of one word and how it can have multiple meanings and be interpreted in so many different ways.

Run

Can you *run* to the store for me?

Can you *run* this computer?

Can you *run* the five-hundred-yard dash?

Can you *run* in the next council election?

Can you *run* next month's school fund-raiser?

I helped Elizabeth with her milk *run*.

They printed five hundred copies of the office schedule in the first *run*.

My mother has a *run* in her nylon stockings.

There is a *run* on air conditioners now.

It was a long *run*.

We do not add together the meanings of individual words in a sentence to get the meaning of the whole. We can't rely on potential meaning. We can only know what a word means when we use it in context. Grammatical context within the sentence: the first five sentences signal *verb*, so it is easier to limit the meaning of *run*.

Semantic context within the sentence: In saying *run the school fund-raiser,* I know it means "manage." Where *run* is the *verb*, I need the noun that comes after it rather than before.

Situational, pragmatic context: *it was a long run* could mean many things.

Schematic context: Experiences and knowledge that I bring to the text enable my interpretation to be broad or narrow.

Life and living require more than mere surface viewings too. We must have more than a single perspective on something to understand and respond to each moment's potential. We can't rely on one experience either. We can only grow in wisdom and grace when we live in context, learning to participate unselfishly without ego, without power's lies, without the false self. We need others, as true companions on the journey, to help us mirror our truth, dissipate the world's manipulations and manage our honest discoveries of life.

Experience and knowledge can be garnered by awareness within life events, as well as by reading/studying scripture, varied spiritual writings, ponderings, musings, poems, and/or songs and by spending time making them personally relevant.

May the meaning and purpose of your life become clear as you accept yourself just as you are and accept others just as they are too. Yes, to be kind, to give up the battles, to trust, to dream, to respect everyone and everything, and to grasp the joy of the journey—there lies happiness and purpose. Most of the problems we face are not to be solved. Most of our journey is to learn that it is not our job to resolve problems. It is our discovery to understand that we are not the center of anything. We are the object of God's love, the beloved.

It takes a lifetime to gather enough meaning, unless you start your journey work early.

If you are in the beginning stages of life, you are lucky!

If you are in the later stages of your life, it's never too late to live abundantly, and you should joyfully seek out those in the beginning stages of life so they know of the journey before it is mere memory.

Elucidation is the motivation, not preaching or lecturing. Things that may have toppled my life may be insignificant in someone else's life. Battles that I have had to fight in my life may be mediocre incidents in the life of another standing before me.

But do not doubt for a moment that all must face battles and wage war within.

Becoming more is a surrender of self, and surrendering self is indeed a battle for everyone!

Even our Old Testament Israelites struggled with surrender and with narrow worlds. Pharaoh was already near when the Israelites looked up and saw that the Egyptians were on the march in pursuit of them. In great fright, they cried out to the Lord. And they complained to Moses, "Were there no burial places in Egypt that you had to bring us out here to die in the desert? Why did you do this to us? Why did you bring us out of Egypt? Did we not tell you this in Egypt, when we said, 'Leave us alone. Let us serve the Egyptians'? Far better for us to be slaves of the Egyptians than to die in the desert." But Moses answered the people, "Fear not! Stand your ground, and you will see the victory the Lord will win for you today. These Egyptians whom you see today you will never see again. The Lord himself will fight for you; you have only to keep still." Then the Lord said to Moses, "Why are you crying out to Me? Tell the Israelites to go forward. And you, lift up your staff and, with hand outstretched over the sea, split the sea in two, that the Israelites may pass through it on dry land." (Exodus 14:10–16)

Sooner or later, we all must give up the fight and, within a trusting surrender, acquiesce to God's work and move beyond who we think we are into a world of greater meaning.

Action Step: (Spiritual Plane)

Ponder being your biggest influence and look deeply into the activities and thought patterns keeping you from the world of greater meaning.

I Sing God's Praise ~ Poem 33

Jesus took a walk with me.
Yes, hand in hand we went.
He showed me all that I could be
and what real trusting meant.

I told Him of my searching
and just how hard I try.
He knows the price of hurting.
He often questioned why.

But in His search to do God's will
Incarnation freed the earth.
And if I trust and let Him fill
me, there will be new birth.

So I took a walk with Jesus.
He put His hand in mine.
Now it's time to speak of this
and humbly touch on the divine.

With all the souls in ecstasy,
with every human heart
I sing God's praise, all glory be,
I've found my place to start.

I'll speak of God's great glory.
Praise the wonders of God's name.
My life now sings God's symphony
for I've been born again.

"They seemed to be staring into the darkness, but their eyes were watching God." Zora Neale Hurston

Visiting our family member who was in a nursing home became our daily ritual. We'd take tea and a small cake or cookie for happy hour, stay and serve the dinner trays in the dining room, sit together in the evening and help settle her in bed for the night. Right away, I noticed a poor woman in the next room who just sat in her big chair every day. I would always take a walk down the hall to visit with Dorothy because her son lived in Ireland and she never had any visitors. Dorothy had huge framed portraits on every inch of wall space in her room. She was an artist! All I had to say was, "Dorothy, this painting is beautiful!" and she would break into the detailed story of the subject she had painted there. She told me that she lost her house when her husband passed away and the son sold most of her work. She was given a few paintings to keep in her room but all of her possessions were gone. Her son was obviously gone too.

Dorothy was stripped of everything and forgotten. Her wonderful husband, her home, her possessions, her treasures, her opportunities to use her gifts and talents to bless others and even her son belonged in her past. Her beautiful face had the innocent emptiness of a small child told to sit and not move. For just the time spent during our visits, Dorothy's pure, undiluted delight to share radiated from her being. She never complained. In her darkest times, she found the invitation to let go of a God of her own making for the God of incomprehensible mystery. She said her time was holy and her days were blessed because she had uninterrupted days to remember being loved and being happy. My days were blessed, too, because I knew that I was able to hug God twice a day there and it absolutely changed me.

I pray you will find confidence and direction in your journaling. We are all the same in God's eyes. We change and become more when we choose to change. Opposite poles of belief systems move between every event in everyone's journey. It is becoming aware of choices, experiences, and negative influences or positive influences in our life that I speak of. How we process, pray, and participate in our abundant, holy NOW is what can change our lives and impact our world.

There is no beginning. There is no end. Eternally growing and becoming more of God's abundance is our personal power source, and it is ever present. Every moment provides everything we need to be complete if we but realize that participation is right here and right now.

What we think, speak, and act upon creates our experiences. Realizations of such power within will balance our being, trigger forward-moving activities and create peace in our progress.

Thank yourself for pursuit of love's energies, heart's abilities to forgive and be happy, and mind's potential to choose abundance. Hug your magnificent self and become a companion on the journey, where everything you long to know is revealed, where everything you need is accessible, and where everyone you love reflects incarnation back into your life.

In my times of morning meditation, leading into contemplation, I choose to love myself into the overflow of perfect and complete abundance, and I invite you to be forever involved in your journey of surrender. Our journey is in knowing we all must surrender in order to confidently conquer and ultimately transcend our physical and mental planes to reach the spiritual plane's joy in our NOW. Meditation is a inward tool where our participation brings pure joy.

Meditation, like healthy eating and mindful exercise, can be a whole body experience when practiced faithfully. This relaxing practice helps us to get in touch with our inner self and find our focus to better develop a sense of balance in life. To pray is your choice. It is not something you have to do. It becomes your life-line, your center, your unshakable joy on the journey.

Let's think about some of the benefits of a faithful meditation practice.

One of the most obvious physical plane benefits of meditating is relaxation. Meditation time invites us to quiet our mind, forget our stress, and truly be present in the moments of our NOW. This mental plane focus obviously helps to encourage relaxation and presence. The less I focus on what's going to happen in the future, what happened in the past, and/or my imminent stressors, and the more I focus on my meditation practices the calmer I will feel.

Meditation has been used for centuries to reduce stress, stimulate relaxation and surface joy and deep gratitude. Jesus often went off to a place of his own to pray.

Being self-aware is a crucial quality to personal success, sincere humility and being an overall good, happy person. Meditation encourages me to reflect inwardly and that focus on my inner-self opens the mental and spiritual planes to better influence my journey on this physical plane. A faithful morning meditation practice improves my self-awareness and that allows me to correct any errors I make or fix character flaws that may challenge my NOW. Being honest will influence my perspective to be a better person in all the "roles" played out in the rest of my day. It can and will always improve my focus. True meditation requires great focus and control; it forces me to spend a designated amount of time in the absolute present, in self-reflection and in a treasured state of empty. The more I deepen my meditation times, the better balance I can achieve in my life. Time dedicated to self-reflection allows me to reach a level of understanding and awareness that helps me to be a better and more understanding person. This designated time helps me reach a balance of self-awareness, self-respect, humility, gratitude, confidence and peace. My days are more balanced and productive, proving the time spent in prayer is a gift that quickly becomes a treasure, a pearl of great price. Because meditation can help improve my self-awareness and observance, it can also show me how to become more aware of those around me. I start to notice when my friends and family members feel uncomfortable or I see when they are in pain. I become better at reading the general mood and energy of the room. I am better able to adjust myself to match that level and better accommodate those around me without unconsciously reacting to situations.

Meditation will help us relax, refocus our mind, get in touch with our inner-self and find a purpose-filled balance to live freely and fully in the NOW.

The more you meditate, the more you will stay in tune with your mind, your body and your journey. This will help you to better understand yourself and others around you. It is your source of power within that will boost your awareness of living in the NOW and be your avionics to constantly keep you on course and present in your NOW.

Action Step: (Physical Plane)

When you pause to pray, ask for all you desire and need to be open and present NOW. My poem here can be your meditation starter and that will end our time with quiet prayer.

<u>Keeper of the New Day ~ Poem 34</u>

Keeper of the new day, unlock the daily treasure
and release the energy that fills every being.

Keeper of the new day, Your touch is beyond all knowing.
Filled with a great wonder, I will trace Your path across the hours.

In only a moment, just the shadows will remain.
Oh, life of the new day, I long for Your friendship.

And I shall be here in prayer again tomorrow.
On the edge of the night, I shall watch for Your coming.

Keeper of the new day, bring again
the colors that blend the beauty of all the living.

Bring again rewards for all anticipations and expectations of ever and only
finding You.

My Destiny ~ Day 32 ~ Spiritual Plane

My Open Meditation:

How do I get my heart to focus on the divine when its sole purpose is to keep me alive in flesh?

How do I get my soul to focus on the human when its sole purpose is to keep me alive in spirit?

Two questions. Seemingly absurd.
A paradigm, a paradox, yet precisely corresponding.
A whole-body person, in communion with all creation, living to activate the inherent spirit realm.

Present for all. Seen and experienced by few.
The offering of a simplistic yet striking delineation of lived faith life.
Gifts of God.
Wholly positive in perspective.
Message of truth.

To meet the Creator on the road of life.
To see Jesus, the Christ, in the breaking of the bread.
All-pervading joy!
Unreservedly uniting heart and soul in a most effective of apostolic affirmations.

To accomplish my allotted task of becoming, I must freely touch a more basic response to life.

To love in the moment.
To show a keen awareness of the layers of my life, the meaning of my living, the responses of willing participation in a total faith occupation.

Truly seeking unconditional readiness in the now, You bestow on me, oh God, the certitude that heart and soul, divine and human, overwhelms me until I allow You near.

Life challenges me. Love pivots me.
You shepherd me home.

Home is where I find that my heart overflows, my soul soars, my person professes that it is my choice that my will belongs to You.

So it is in the stark contrast of a heart soaring and a soul feeling deeply that rewards are released upon those faithful companions on the journey.

A living conundrum communicates the connecting contradictions of heart and soul.

My free will. I choose You in my NOW! Amen.

To use this as a source to deepen your meditation time, simply pause and ponder my sentences.

There is no right or wrong, No purposeful flow intended for you to grasp.

It's about moving through the struggle to become safe and confident in the emptying.

"You were born with wings, why prefer to crawl through life?" Rumi

"The miracle of your existence calls for celebration every day." Oprah Winfrey

Let's continue by singing the very first song I wrote called Composed for You.

Composed For You

1. Let me sing a lit-tle song of praise___ to You, Lord.
2. Ev-'ry-one must learn___ to sing a song for You, Lord,
3. When we learn to sing our song, it's true, we give You praise, Lord.
4. When our Word In-car-nate___ came to dwell with us. He

1. Let me sing and bless___ Your great and awe-some name.___
2. stand-ing with their head up high___ or when things seem blue.___
3. When we sing to-geth-er all the world's in har-mo-ny.___
4. sang His per-fect song of praise and said, "Now fol-low Me.___ Make

1. Ev-'ry-thing I say,___ ev-'ry-thing I do___
2. Ev-'ry-where we turn,___ ev-'ry-thing we do___
3. Ev-'ry-thing we say,___ ev-'ry-thing we do___
4. ev-'ry-thing you say,___ ev-'ry-thing you do___ (To final ending)

1. longs to be a song of praise com-posed and sung___ for You.___
2. must be-come a song of praise com-posed and sung___ for You.___
3. then be-comes a song of praise com-posed and lived___ for You.___

Final Ending

4. join My per-fect song of praise and I'll live on in you."___

December 25, 1968 Words and Music by Patricia Jean Smithyman-Zito.

www.LivingInTheNowBook.com/music

Moving deeper through the mental plane:

Faithfully completing our course corrections has brought us to a deeper place. Following the suggestions throughout the book have brought us to a new place. We are finding the places and things we have not thought about or have avoided for a long time. This is reward! Awareness of joy!

Awareness of the hidden meaning of life, now conscious of the feelings deep in my soul of yearning, desiring, and hoping that there is so much more meaning and purpose to all this lifetime we must go through, beyond science, beyond my senses, invisible yet totally real, enables me to sing, smile and surrender. We can't afford not to claim our benison, our blessing.

Life in the physical plane is too short! Mastery of the mental plane comes too late! Our destiny is forever in the spiritual plane, but it begins here and now.

Discovering the confidence of a spiritual plane understanding, while walking in the physical plane, gives me an unshakable faith in the goodness and purpose of my journey. My attention to life and love blends the three planes and establishes my relationship with all that unfolds. Realizations of living in my NOW enables me to reclaim my journey with joyous appreciations of being alive.

NOW is the time to embrace who we are in God and to celebrate with everything we are in Christ! Spirit is our greatest gift, and wisdom is our treasure. Strength is found while traveling as companions on the journey, and we choose to sing our song of praise, healing our wounded hearts and broken spirits and bringing love, peace, hope, and joy to our physical and mental planes as we soar to our spiritual destiny.

God's Grace ~ Poem 35

Putting pen to this paper I simply must do.
I have a message to share with you.

God, in great mercy, has set me free.
Forgiveness and peace I can finally see.

Not by my virtue, but by God's endless grace,
have I found my way to this holier place.

The depth of God's presence and patience for me
has enabled a proper perspective to be.

Demands that concerned me, I now must declare,
hold little value since I've replaced them with prayer.

In the presence of God, I know only what's true,
and I humbly try here to explain it to you.

In God's presence is freedom from things of this earth.
Just commit with me now to new spiritual birth.

Action Step: (Mental Plane)

Sing of understanding faithfulness and give all the "Glory and Honor to God" with me!

March 14, 2000 Music and Words by Patricia Jean Smithyman-Zito.

www.LivingInTheNowBook.com/music

Once the truth of our belovedness in God is realized and actualized, so is our choice within it.

Whenever our mind imagines all of creation incarnating God's presence among us; whenever our spirit remembers being with God from all eternity; whenever we understand how our soul radiates grace, peace, mercy, and love into our every action, we are free. It is a seeming paradox to be free within our surrender to obey and follow the One who has told us He is the way, the truth and the life. But unlike following the "rules" of the Old Testament image of a God who was feared, we follow the beatitudes of the New Testament image of a God who is loved and who loves us radically, even in our moments of not choosing what we've now come to know as good.

Developing a relationship with the Whole of Holy requires me to be consciously present with feelings and thoughts that are authentically mine. I must choose to live such an existential presence to the Body of Christ that I can then risk living with myself as I truly am. When I am open to the needs of this world and its totality, to the power found in selfless love, to God's ever-Incarnate Presence in my NOW, at the level of body-person reflective awareness, I can overcome, acknowledge, and even use my weaknesses to encounter Life and change the world right within my NOW.

Every moment is a risk, a new beginning, a new surrender and a new time to pray. Will we be perfect?

No, but we are better able to stay the course using our tools, planning our days and listening.

Perfection isn't the issue. Faithfulness is the call and love is the journey.

We are no longer in the physical or mental planes of doubt, worry, and broken spirits.

This is what we know and grow to believe:

Blending my physical and mental planes during quiet time/meditation time exposes my false self, my negative thinking and my stressors to face my own truth. I believe there is a new understanding of how my mind is the source of all stress from outside sources brought to bear upon my body. Every thought of effort in my mind, of whatever sort, transmits a motor impulse to my body; and every such impulse causes a deviation from my "normal" and lessens the sensitiveness at the center of my being to flow copiously.

If I want to have perfect energy flow, I must minimize stress in my mind. Mental strain of any kind always produces conscious or unconscious strain and if the strain takes the form of effort, chaos is always produced. On the mental plane, there is only one cure for all of my varied stressors; relaxation during prayer.

During relaxation and prayer, we actually face our truth on the mental plane and learn to surrender to the events on our physical plane, eliminating stress and its effects. Our physical plane is largely influenced by our thoughts. When our thoughts are normal, that is, not influenced by any outside excitement or strain, the circulation in our brain is normal, the supply of blood to our optic nerve and our visual centers are normal, and our vision is perfect. When our thoughts are abnormal, our circulation is disturbed, the supply of blood to our optic nerve and visual centers is altered, and our vision is impaired physically, mentally and spiritually.

I think thoughts that disturb my circulation and lower my power whether I am aware of it or not! I can also consciously think thoughts that will restore normal circulation and thereby improve my efforts to "see" both literally and figuratively.

When a disturbing thought is replaced by one that relaxes, my squint disappears, the double vision and the errors of refraction are corrected, my weak knees become strong, my pounding heart resumes its normal beating, my labored breathing becomes a normal, deep breath and my mind clearly speaks my unadulterated truth.

These thoughts are pure and not influenced by the ingredients of my life. The noise of my physical plane ceases, all of my ego demands dissolve, prideful selfishness and dualistic thinking stressors are silenced and an awakening is accomplished. This happens as soon as I am able to develop and secure mental control through relaxing techniques used during prayer and quiet time.

The cause of any error, any pressure, every misguided concept my mind can conjure is seen as being simply a thought. That is profound awareness! It is often a wrong thought, too! My perspective improvement is as quick as the thought that relaxes and enables my refocus of truth in my NOW. In a fraction of a second, the highest degrees of stressors are corrected!

Start simply but be diligent. If relaxation during prayer is only momentary, the correction is momentary. When it becomes permanent, the correction is permanent. Relaxation during prayer blends my physical and mental planes and allows my energy, my perspectives, my hope and my spiritual plane to flow freely and productively as I move through each moment of my day.

This is the secret to making each day my best! My treasure to always live fully in the NOW!

It's about the journey, and it is all in God's plan to heal us, love us, and teach us of the breadth, depth, and height of loving! We can do this! God manifests as Incarnate Body Person within the very forces of the physical plane and the mental plane and reveals that Emmanuel, God, is with us and is our security, our path and our promise.

But now, thus says the Lord, who created you, O Jacob, and formed you O Israel: "Fear not, for I have redeemed you; I have called you by name: you are Mine. When you pass through the water, I will be with you; in the rivers you shall not drown. When you walk through fire, you shall not be burned; the flames shall not consume you. For I am the Lord, your God, the Holy One." (Isaiah 43:1-3)

Because you are precious and glorious in My eyes and because I love you, fear not, for I am with you. (Isaiah 43:4-5)

_____

_____

_____

_____

_____

_____

_____

_____

_____

_____

_____

_____

_____

_____

_____

_____

_____

_____

A Brand New Day

April 28, 1973 Words and Music by Patricia Jean Smithyman-Zito.

www.LivingInTheNowBook.com/music

Action Step: (Spiritual Plane)

Faithfulness is the call and love, the journey. Write of your journey to let go of much while taking up so much more. Therein lies the secret for making each day your best day. Write of your spiritual birth.

Extend Your Hand ~ Day 34 ~ Tough Love!

"Your task is not to seek for love, but merely to seek and find all the barriers within yourself that you have built against it." Rumi

Will we always have love, peace and meaning in everything we do? Yes, if we remember the spark within us, the love around us, and the purpose for which we are on this journey. The need to find barriers within will always keep us working our flight plan and making course corrections. Seek inner space and deep work, course correct your personal journey work and seek community/family/society for bringing incarnational love to our world together.

Perhaps attending celebrations of Liturgy or Eucharistic adoration, being an associate or member of a Catholic/Christian order/ community, spending time in personal/private/communal prayer, walking a labrynith, praying the rosary and traditional prayers or the Liturgy of the Hours, or doing some type of spiritual reading and sharing the journey's experiences with others will deepen our faith.

Putting time and talents together to be of service within church or community circles is a time of promised personal giving but always becomes a time of receiving too. Even adding varied types of fasting can keep us in touch with our blessings and deepen our awareness to love in each gifted moment.

A grateful heart is a happy heart. A happy heart finds the benison in every moment, and in every person. That respectful foundation enables grace and openness to the holy order of living in abundance. The real person within is then able to bridge the gap into the spiritual plane.

What foundations will you or do you have to keep your faith, hope and love strong?

Are you adding healthy food choices, consistent exercise, personal growth material, and more quiet times of prayer into your schedule?

Just because I haven't mentioned things a 2nd or 3rd time doesn't mean they are not still on your plate, right? Speaking of "plate," I gave you 10 days to build your elimination diet framework: *Become an Expert ~ Day 4 ~ Mulling Over the Meaning.* That means you've completely changed your lifestyle by now and are feeling healthier and happier because of eating well for the past month, right? Truthfully, my dear companion on the journey, if you are simply reading and not engaging, your NOW is not likely to change to the levels desired.

Time for review and course corrections:

_____

_____

_____

_____

_____

_____

_____

_____

Action Step: (Physical Plane)

We've been working for 34 days already! Congratulations to you for pushing forward to establish a life of loving unconditionally in your NOW!

Oh, the 40 days of Lent! Much achieved by Day 34! I can't wait for Easter and Resurrection's new NOW.

If you have disciplined your 3 planes with each day's disclosures you are a saint! Literally!

It is a good time to listen to my song "Why I'm Sure" because life is a challenge and "becoming more on the journey" is surely a choice. Most take a lifetime to realize their gift of presence in their NOW. Love yourself enough to find the barriers to being free and remove them. Let's sing before you devote time and use tough love to meet the challenges in today's action step. Then come back to today's musings to consciously connect with pertinent ponderings here that help you break down barriers on your physical plane to build you up more.

Why I'm Sure

Guitar: Capo 3 Play G

♩=135

Harmony
Melody

1. I'm____ not sure I know ex - act - ly why I'm here; well,
2. Look____ at me, dis - turbed and e - ven quite per - plexed; well,
3. There may be times of doubt but nev - er times of com - plete de - spair for
4. Take all I am and all that I will ev - er be. I

1. I'm not e - ven sure, I'll be a - live to
2. I'm not e - ven sure, I'll live to see the
3. when I stop to look a - bout I find that You are
4. pro - mise you my love from now un - til e -

1. love to - mor - row. All I real - ly know,____ Lord,
2. sun to - mor - row. All I real - ly know,____ Lord,
3. pres - ent there, and once a - gain I sing,____ Lord,
4. ter - ni - ty. I'll sing Your song each day,____ Lord,

1. is I de - pend up - on____ You.____
2. is I de - pend up - on____ You.____
3. how I de - pend up - on____ You.____
4. as I de - pend up - on____ You.____

February 19, 1969 Words and Music by Patricia Jean Smithyman-Zito.

www.LivingInTheNowBook.com/music

Being in Love ~ Day 35 ~ Self Worth

Being in love is something, isn't it? The world is surely seen differently and it's summer in the middle of winter! You can fall in love with God, Jesus, your faith-life, your spouse or significant other, members of your family, your doctor, your neighbor, your pet, your worthy cause, your job, yourself and even your NOW. You can wake up in the morning and fall in love over and over again. I mean it! Nothing can compare to the awareness or raise your physical, mental and spiritual vibrations of abundance like when you are head over heels in love! You can float on those vibrations every minute of every day. That includes the days when you can't seem to figure out why you're here or what you are called to be in this specific NOW. You stay in love because you have taken the scheduled times to sit with your flight-plan and visit your inner rooms to consciously and meditatively master the integration of your 3 planes. It is in your mental plane that facing the truth enables you to discipline your personal agenda beyond yourself. You are so worth this journey, my friend!

So, everything falls into place because I am in love with and cooperating within God's plan.

Problems still seem challenging, but solvable and quite trivial when I depend on God, trust God's coordinates and live within my promise to love. That is why I am sure even when I am not so sure. That's how Jesus, the Incarnate Word, could leave His perfect Heaven and choose to become human, coming to earth looking like us. Jesus was so perfectly human that he was divine. Jesus said yes to show us how to transform ourselves back into our original image and likeness of God, and it is always a choice.

Falling in love with being perfectly human so that we become divine is the secret to making each day our best! Thank-You, Jesus!

How has mastering your thoughts helped you to be in love? What mental plane work will help you to unconditionally fall in love with everyone, everything and every NOW? That is how we find heaven here on earth, NOW!

_____

_____

_____

_____

_____

_____

_____

_____

_____

_____

_____

Going deeper:

The students at Incarnate Word Academy in Parma Heights, Ohio, have made this their school song. They sing with such enthusiasm and excitement! Our young are so very refreshing!

March 25, 2008 Text and Music by Patricia Jean Smithyman-Zito.

www.LivingInTheNowBook.com/music

My prayer for you, dear companion on the journey, is that you quickly come to understand that lacking wisdom, self-knowledge and a disciplined NOW causes us to frame our lives incorrectly.

When we cannot see our true self and understand our dualistic thinking, we cannot see the reality of our journey and we cannot fall head over heels in love with our every NOW.

Conquering the physical plane chaos and honestly dwelling in the truth of the mental plane, we transform our NOW moments into spiritual plane gifts.

"Good God, the creator of light and darkness, You who move the sun and the stars, move us into the place of light, a light so large that it will absorb all the darkness." Fr. Richard Rohr, OFM

Our course corrections must be unpacked constantly within our NOW.

Here are course correction reminder tips to ponder again for each of the three planes:

Physical Plane Tips – Course Corrections #2

- We've been watching meals lately, right?
- I try not to eat the same thing within a three day rotation. For example, my Nana Anna wanted oatmeal for breakfast every morning and my mom eats a sandwich every day for lunch. Your body needs variety to get the many different values of nutrition necessary to feed your body at the cellular level.
- So shake things up a bit and live big by eating lots of different things! Be creative, eat lots of colors and remember that God made us to live forever. Our body is a miracle happening within every second! We can support our physical plane and know that our cells heal when given the right things to work with in a healthy environment. Sit and sip with that thought for a few days!

- For more information, healthy tips and free resources, visit us at **www.LivingInTheNowBook.com/physical**

For your new NOW, remind yourself that your body loves Mother Nature's natural foods with little or no processing. Lowering your simple carbohydrates intake from your diet is a course correction your body needs to then burn fat for energy because cheap carbs are no longer a choice.

Without a constant flow of cheap carbs that the body would generally turn into sugar, the blood sugar falls to normal and insulin level starts regulating. A regulated insulin level allows lipolysis to take place. Lipolysis is basically the process where your body releases fat stores to be then burned in the form of energy. By lowering any number of cheap carbs in your body, you will start burning fat for fuel! Simply focus on the unprocessed and real foods which have been around for thousands and thousands of years.

Here is a quick guide to targeting the foods that our ancestors had access to.

- Lean meats – beef, veal, venison, lamb, chicken, bison, etc. (try eating grass-fed versions of these)
- Fish – salmon, tilapia, bass, etc. (realize that farm-raised fish is not included here)
- Seafood (easy on all types of shell-fish because most are scavengers)
- Eggs (eggs have a lot more benefits if they are organic and from free-range chickens)
- Vegetables – (raw, steamed and baked)
- Berries and the less sugary fruits are good
- Nuts – not too much (avoid peanuts that are full of fungus)
- Natural oils – olive, coconut and avocado oils

Mental Plane Tips - Course Corrections #2

- How can I think about my thinking and actually feel what I am feeling?
- Our standing across the room to observe ourselves gives us a great opportunity to see who we are and how we behave/react.
- As a child, my parents spoke to me about my actions. In school, as the teacher, I spoke to my students about their actions. As an adult, I can speak to myself about my actions, too.
- The key is to avoid negatives and criticisms and putting ourselves down. There's enough of that passing through us, from all around us to last a hundred lifetimes.
- So, let's mirror our actions to the actions of Jesus when He walked the earth.
- A few years ago, a saying circulated and people were wearing bands on their wrists with letters *WWJD* on them. The band was a mental plane reminder and the letters stood for *W*hat *W*ould *J*esus *D*o in this situation, this NOW? *WWJD* can be a daily course correction for us all!
- For more information, motivations and great resources, visit us at **www.LivingInTheNowBook.com/mental**

Spiritual Plane Tips – Course Corrections #2

- How long are your morning and evening *"sit and sip"* times lasting?
- For as much as I want to journal about my changes, the *"sit and sip"* times are to be a quiet emptying, a being still, a kind of surrendering time.
- To make that happen, you really can't think about being empty, still or quiet. You just have to be. We are human *be*-ings. We are not human *do*-ings or human *think*-ings!
- Jesus went off to pray often, saying *"Follow Me."*

- Squeeze another *"sit and sip"* time into your routine. A few more moments spent being *present* will actually provide you with what you need to use the rest of your day's time well.
- For more spiritual inspiration, motivation and great prayer resources, visit us at **www.LivingInTheNowBook.com/spiritual**

Action Step: (Mental Plane)

Remember and repeat daily:
Happiness reigns in my life, my home, my workplace, when I give substance to my thoughts, feelings and needs. Yes, when I actually spend time in my heart and my head, I realize that my world is a happy place. I truly do enjoy living in each "NOW." When I walk through my front door, I feel a palpable sense of peace and genuine love overwhelming me. There is no place in the world I would rather be than in my happy home. The soundtrack of my life is filled with laughter and joy. In everything I do, I make it a point to focus and have fun. I turn any situation into a happy situation by shifting my point of view. Sometimes I laugh because things are funny; other times I just laugh at myself. I can laugh at my fears and even at my mistakes because I am defined by so much more. I refuse to take life so seriously that my joy disappears. Instead, I look for reasons to smile and celebrate. Happiness reigns in my life and in my NOW moments because I am slow to anger and quick to forgive. That starts with me, in my NOW, and then it easily extends to work, family and friends. My loved ones are happy because they know I love them unconditionally. Joy rules my responses and joy rules the atmosphere of my life because love has cast out fear. The people in my life are happy because I model refreshing, little changes that focus on having a positive attitude and a grateful heart. This awareness frees all of us from the destructive effects of ego's selfishness. I model for my loved ones how to speak to others with kindness and compassion because I have fallen in love with living in the NOW.

Today, I choose to reject Ego's selfishness and embrace love. I course correct to shift my point of view so I can see my family, my coworkers, my friends, and my true self in every moment, through eyes of compassion and with a happy heart of gratitude.

Self-reflection questions for larger course corrections:

1. What is the soundtrack of my daily life?
2. How can I model a positive attitude to my loved ones, to everyone I meet?
3. What course corrections are bringing the changes that are becoming habits:
   On my physical plane?

   On my mental plane?

   On my spiritual plane?

All the deep work today enables me to know my journey at a level of self-awareness I can then take out to all those I meet. Without many words I can impact my world just by being in love.

Can You Tell Me, Lord?

September 3, 1973 Words and Music by Patricia Jean Smithyman-Zito.

www.LivingInTheNowBook.com/music

Jesus knew who He was because He spent time with Himself and with His Father in prayer.

"The authentic self is the Soul made visible."
Sarah Ban Breathnach

- Working on my "self" is a huge task.
- We've spent our whole lives becoming everything everyone tells us we should be.
- Everything speaks of being the best we can be, and rightly so, but for now, let's just work on knowing who we really are today.
- Nobody is perfect. That is okay!
- The task at hand is to find and love my "true self" and to know who I am is what this journey is all about.

"While I wrote for two years, Simple Abundance underwent an extraordinary metamorphosis, as did I. On the page every morning, spirituality, authenticity, and creativity converged into an intimate search for Wholeness. I began writing about eliminating clutter and ended up on a safari of the self and Spirit. No one is more astonished by this than I am." Sarah Ban Breathnach

When we look within, we find God. Jesus took upon Himself all of the self-centered forces within the human race, too, when the Word became flesh. That is Incarnation. Jesus lived life in a completely other-centered way to show us the power of God within us. We come to know God because Jesus became human and the God-Man bore the world to bear witness of unselfish love. I want to live in communion with God as Jesus did. Therefore, I must know Jesus to know God.

Then, the Physical Plane is my journey, the Mental Plane is my truth, and the Spiritual Plane is my power source. We have uncovered the secret to making each day our best.

Let's let Jesus sing this next song to us.

I am ev - 'ry where._____

4. You must work hard with each new day. And you will find My peace, My

love will stay._____ I have come to you, the Word - Made-Flesh.

Now com-plete My work on earth, go tell the rest._____ Tell them

I am the way.   Tell them I am the Way.   I am the way.

August 2, 1974 Words and Music by Patricia Jean Smithyman-Zito.
www.LivingInTheNowBook.com/music

Jesus is the way. Jesus is the bread of life. We are challenged to discover Jesus in our every NOW. As our journey deepens, our belief system expands beyond walls, rules and earthly demands. Where does your belief system fall?

_____

_____

_____

_____

_____

_____

_____

_____

_____

_____

O = All strings are open
♩=130 Joyfully

Bread Must Be Broken

1. Soft - ly - and - gent - ly You beck - on___ from the shore.
2. Soft - ly and gent - ly You beck - on___ on the road.
3. Soft - ly and gent - ly You beck - on___ us to play.
4. Soft - ly and gent - ly You beck - on___ when we fail.

1. You ask that we take and eat. We long for more!
2. You ask that we in - vite You in, ease our hea - vy load.
3. You ask that___ we should live Your joy - ful way.
4. You reach out and___ heal our wounds. We are so frail.

1. Bread to be bro - ken! Wine to be shared! Come, re - ceive!
2. Bread to be bro - ken! Wine to be shared! Recog - nize Me!
3. Bread to be bro - ken! Wine to be shared! Fol - low Me!
4. Bread that is bro - ken! Wine that is shared! Come, be healed!

5. Soft - ly and gent - ly, I call you to u - ni - ty! With each en - coun - ter

you are chal - lenged to dis - cov - er Me. Bread must be bro - ken! Wine must be

shared! End - less - ly!___ Bread must be bro - ken! Wine must be shared! End - less - ly!!!

July 18, 1976 Words and Music by Patricia Jean Smithyman-Zito.

www.LivingInTheNowBook.com/music

I believe in one God, the Father almighty, maker of heaven and earth, of all things visible and invisible. I believe in one Lord Jesus Christ, the Only Begotten Son of God, born of the Father before all ages. God from God, Light from Light, true God from true God, begotten, not made, consubstantial with the Father; through Him all things were made. For us and for our salvation Jesus came down from heaven and by the Holy Spirit was incarnate of the Virgin Mary, and became man. For our sake, Jesus was crucified under Pontius Pilate, suffered death and was buried, and rose again on the third day in accordance with the Scriptures. Jesus ascended into heaven and is seated at the right hand of the Father. He will come again in glory to judge the living and the dead and His kingdom will have no end. I believe in the Holy Spirit, the Lord, the giver of life, who proceeds from the Father and the Son, who with the Father and the Son is adored and glorified, who has spoken through the prophets. I believe in one, holy, Catholic and apostolic Church. I confess one Baptism for the forgiveness of sins and I look forward to the resurrection of the dead and the life of the world to come. Amen.

Action Step: (Spiritual Plane)

Where do you stand in your belief system? How do you use your belief system to unfold the love of Jesus and enable the finding of God? A simple phrase that Jesus used as He taught the Our Father works for me. "Your will be done on earth as it is in heaven."

Let's go back to Jesus. Everybody knows this man! Sing along and write in your journal after the song!

Everybody Knows This Man

1. What's that He's preach - in'? He's the car - pen - ter's son.
2. We want Him cru - ci - fied. Our work won't be done.
3. Yes, the peo - ple have joined with Him. What a high price He paid.
4. He has ris - en tri - umph - ant - ly. Lord of hea - ven and earth.

1. Why that's false teach - ing. Fa - ther, Your will be done.
2. The people will join with Him. Fa - ther, Your will be done.
3. As one body we join with Him. Fa - ther, Your will be done.
4. His cry rings out end - lessly. Fa - ther, Your will be done.

January 28, 1975 Words and Music by Patricia Jean Smithyman-Zito.

www.LivingInTheNowBook.com/music

Anna is precious, spiritual, loving, joyous, peaceful and happy. She is bubbly, smiling, helpful and prayerfully grateful for her many blessings. She lives her life as significantly as any would hope to do. She is more involved than a scientist or a thinker who is curious about the world around her. She is much more involved with the outside world than the inner world, but ironically, is far less threatened. She is what is generally classed as magnanimous, knowledgeable, able to reason out any problem and very perceptive about the world. She not only lives in this world, she has studied it and has an accurate and realistic view of the world. She is a researcher at heart, although not necessarily in books. She likes to get involved physically, mentally and spiritually, and all the while learning all there is to learn from everything. She has an outsider's perceptiveness about the world.

She is very objective. She never seeks leadership, but, when pressed into it, can be very forceful and headstrong in what she believes and treasures and wants others to have, too.

Anna believes in love and spiritual awakenings and strategizes constantly to show others how to be more open to God's presence and life's good.

Without too much formal education, she has an amazing amount of self-taught knowledge because she is so very open to what others have to say or offer.

Anna is spoken of highly as being wise and perceptive, seeing life's journey as the lifeblood of the gifts given without limit. She's able to synthesize information and experiences to truly make informed decisions which can often be seen as annoyingly analytic. As a kind of robot on a mission, she could be almost impossible to connect with intimately, being far more concerned with the how and why things are happening than the way they are with "us" in them. Anna is perceptive, intelligent and genuinely loving. Others, who are her friends and companions on the journey, remind her to stop long enough to hear the chimes in her heart. Together they search for truth, awareness, presence, understanding and love. It is because of how their relationships mold them into someone new that an amazing amount of creativity, contentment, joy and peace flows to a deepening of their relationships with each other and with their God.

Anna is constantly changing when she connects to another person and learns to put aside the expectations. She experiences life with others, discovers how trusting works and becomes ever more open to God's revelations as she journeys to more in her ever evolving NOW.

Like Anna, we are building relationships with each other as companions on the journey should!

Look for more information about connecting in the back of the book!

We are God's people and we give thanks for each other, pray for each other and help each other to grow in the NOW.

We Are God's People

April 29, 2010 Words and Music by Patricia Jean Smithyman-Zito.

www.LivingInTheNowBook.com/music

A Blessing ~ Poem 36

Thank you for your presence,
for your words so freely given.

It is for me, a blessing
sent by God through you from heaven.

We need to hear these positives,
no matter great or small.

Our momentary givings
are recognized by a few or none at all.

A kindness in a word or deed
is an everlasting treasure

That goes on creating goodness
at its source. It has no measure.

So now I send it back to you.
May you feel you, too, are blessed.

Continue to be positive.
It's life's key to loving best.

Here's your personal invitation.

Let Me Be Your Friend

April 18, 1989 Words and Music by Patricia Jean Smithyman-Zito.
www.LivingInTheNowBook.com/music

How can we become friends on this journey? Would a members' chat room be a resource of interest to you? Write of suggestions and ideas to bring to our group by going to www.LivingInTheNowBook.com/journey

_____

_____

_____

_____

_____

_____

_____

Jesus became human to show us how we are made in the image and likeness of God. We are everything ever created. We are a universe. We are eternity. We are the object of God's power, God's endless love. And God desires union. God creates everything, and then everything returns to God.

I'm adding this next song as tribute for all our beloved who have conquered the physical plane and the mental plane and are now enjoying the spiritual plane after returning to God for all eternity. Sing along and celebrate the new NOW that our loved ones in heaven are enjoying.

Walking Beside You

Alternate words verse 3: Living without you, for the rest of my life, I will still be your husband, you will still be my wife.
Alternate words verse 4: join hands with our son / daughter / children.

1. Am I real - ly ex - pec - ted to live with - out you?___ Vs. 2
2. Am I real - ly ex - pec - ted to live with - out you?___ Vs. 3
3. Join hands with our [fami - ly] 'til our jour - ney is through.___ Vs. 4
4. Join hands with our [fami - ly] 'til our jour - ney is through.___ Vs. 5

5. Walk - ing be - side us,___ day af - ter day, our love will grow deep - er in

a spir - it - tual way. Lov - ing you deep - ly though you're

physi - cally gone, God will give us the strength to go on.___

December 15, 1983 Words and Music by Patricia Jean Smithyman-Zito

www.LivingInTheNowBook.com/music

Action Step: (Physical Plane)

Meeting you in prayer each day because the real journey is yours.

"There is no use in one person attempting to tell another what the meaning of life is. It involves too intimate an awareness. A major part of the meaning of life is contained in the very discovering of it. It is an ongoing experience of growth that involves a deepening contact with reality. To speak as though it were an objective knowledge, like the date of the war of 1812, misses the point altogether. The meaning of life is indeed objective when it is reached, but the way to it is by a path of subjectivities. . . . The meaning of life cannot be told; it has to happen to a person." Ira Progoff

Here is a list of tools (suggestions) to incorporate into your daily NOW coordinates to help you stay on course 99% of your flight-journey back to God.

- Meditation/Contemplation
- Mantak Chia Techniques
- Conscious breathing
- Yoga/Chakras/Reflexology
- Massage
- Experience Acupuncture
- Aromatherapy/Essential Oils
- Journal writing/Keeping a gratitude journal
- Intensive Journal (writing dialogues with events, places, relationships, etc. as described by Ira Progoff, M.D.)
- Walking/Running/Lifting
- Painting/Sketching/Coloring
- Playing an instrument/Singing/Dancing
- Shamanic circles
- Examen of consciousness
- Study dreaming
- Look for/identify transformative experiences
- Recognize personal strengths and weaknesses
- Consciously examine pros and cons before decision making
- Find your inner theater
- Take the RHETI inventory test for the enneagram
- Do the MYERS BRIGGS personality test (16personalities.com/free-personality-test)
- Learn new things
- Make something with your hands:
- Clay
- Woodworking
- Crocheting/Needlepoint/Sewing

- Cooking
- Plan meals as a gourmet chef
- Prepare vegetarian meals
- Study eliminating certain foods to see if they disturb your digestive process
- Follow Dash diet (for lowering high blood pressure naturally) or study suggestions used in the Paleo diet, Mediterranean diet or even the Rice diet!
- Try juicing for several days/Incorporate fasting
- Forks Over Knives by Caldwell Esselstyn, M.D.
- Make a retreat
- Create rituals for the Ember days 4 times a year
- Volunteer
- Celebrate an unbirthday

- Join us for so much more at: www.LivingInTheNowBook.com/journey

Realize that free will is a gift.

Raise your hands.
Pray and sing the next song to merge with the Infinite One and live in the confidence of personal prayer as Jesus taught us.

Grateful and Blest

1. I want to know You, God.   I want to love You, God.   I want to serve You more.
2. I choose to praise You, God.   I choose to hon - or You.   I choose to give my love.
3. I am a - stound - ed, God.   I am so hum - bled, God.   I am so grateful and blest.
4. I want to know You, God.   I want to love You, God.   I want to serve You more.

June 6, 2012 Words and Music by Patricia Jean Smithyman-Zito.

www.LivingInTheNowBook.com/music

In this journey, I remind myself, in times of prayer, to be authentic. I must choose the truth in every moment in order to merge with the Infinite One and live in the confidence of God's loving plan. I do not need to understand everything. I do not need to control everything. I only need to know of living fully, with a heart of gratitude, so I can choose to love, honor and praise my way back to union with my beloved. This journey is about taking care of and becoming more of me in me; in God: Almighty, Infinite Person, Creator, Holy One, Spirit, Lover of mine, Incarnate Word.

It is difficult to accept that I must put myself first, but only then am I strong, centered, focused and able to love God, others, and all of creation unconditionally. I must come to know my own importance in my journey because only then am I filled to that abundance of overflowing awareness.

Without guilt, competition, comparisons, pressures to achieve, and other physical and mental plane weavings, I am able to stand as *me*, as I am in my truth, before this God who loves unconditionally.

Yes, now I understand that I am the one who blocks, denies, limits and controls how love overflows. The physical and mental planes overwhelm my remembering of presence and truth available in my NOW. There is the secret we have uncovered because of our faithfulness!

The journey is about remembering presence, union and abundance. Hold a newborn in your arms; you'll remember. Look into the face of a one-year-old who just managed to cross the floor without crawling; you'll remember. Focus on receiving the Eucharist; you'll remember. Hold the hand of your beloved one who is dying; you'll remember. We need to remember presence and our purpose for the journey and allow ourselves to just be. I am simply a human being. You are simply a human being. We've been programmed to believe we are a "human becoming." Get that? Sooner rather than later, strive to just *be*.

The becoming more we struggle with most of our lifetime only happens when we can truly just be. Be ourselves, love ourselves, and give ourselves away because we can.

Thank You, Lord!

July 11, 1969 Words and Music by Patricia Jean Smithyman-Zito.

www.LivingInTheNowBook.com/music

Presence ~ Poem 37

Not so very long ago, in God's time, anyway,
Jesus came to let us know God loves us more and more each day.

He didn't come to take control. He came and walked the land
to teach us of the Golden Rule to walk this journey hand in hand.

So now it's time to stop a while to remember all He said.
God's Word shows us exactly how to live as risen from the dead.

Now you know God's love is real, however hard your way.
May loving others help you feel God's presence with you every day.

Action Step: (Mental Plane)

Operating Vision we have established:

1. Life's three planes of awareness:
   a. Physical Plane
   b. Mental Plane
   c. Spiritual Plane
2. Awareness and integration creates synergy (living fully in the NOW)

Incorporating the three planes into our life-plans/flight coordinates creates a synergy that brings us to a mindfulness of living fully in the NOW.

The Freedom to Choose ~ Day 39 ~ Precious Gifts to Win or Lose

On day 39, we sing of not having all the answers! WOW!

You'd think after all this work we would be ready to cross the finish line on day 40 with the crowds screaming!

We may still have questions and lots of work to do but we can now tap wisdom, grace and self-discipline to move us through the physical and mental planes to live each day as our best day in the spiritual plane.

The amazing truth is that we share all we have discovered by simply living fully in our NOW.

My Precious Gift

November 25, 1985 Words and Music by Patricia Jean Smithyman-Zito.

www.LivingInTheNowBook.com/music

Before we bring our journey together to an end, I want to ask you to inventory your loved ones and write down their names: your grandmother, grandfather, mother, father, husband, wife, children, grandchildren, great-grandchildren, brothers, sisters, nieces, nephews, aunts, uncles, cousins, friends, neighbors, coworkers and prayer partners.

The list will probably need to be on another sheet of paper if you are blessed enough to have a very long list or if you want to really expand this journal idea. If you want to give this some serious thought, please take all the time you need.

Write each name and then write a series of words or even sentences about that person.

You can write about their gifts, talents, and personalities.

Think of their impact on your life, what kind of relationship you have with them, and how much involvement they have in your journey. If the person has passed away, you can still write about them and even write about the involvement they have in your journey because you know they are still kything to you from the spiritual plane.

> Everything written before our time was written for our instruction, that we might derive hope from the lessons of patience and the words of encouragement in the Scriptures. May God, the source of all patience and encouragement, enable you to live in perfect harmony with one another according to the spirit of Christ Jesus, so that with one heart and voice you may glorify God, the Father of our Lord Jesus Christ. Accept one another, then, as Christ accepts you, for the glory of God. (Romans 15:4–7)

When you have your inventory of loved ones completed, with all your adjectives describing them in front of you, write one word describing how they feel about your involvement in their journey, your impact on their life.

Sometime in the near future, spend time with each person in your life. Tell them of your journey, your needs, your hopes, and your love. May God enable you to live in perfect harmony so you may glorify God as true companions on the journey.

> The fruit of the Spirit is love, joy, peace, patient endurance, kindness, generosity, faith, mildness and chastity. Against such there is no law! Those who belong to Christ Jesus have crucified their flesh with its passions and desires. Since we live by the Spirit, let us follow the Spirit's lead. Let us never be boastful, or challenging, or jealous toward one another.
> (Galatians 5:22–26)
>
> "Behold God beholding you and smiling."
> Peter von Bramen, SJ

_____

_____

_____

_____

_____

_____

_____

_____

_____

Going deeper:

My job as teacher, musician, interpreter, whatever, is "the job," but it is not my "work." My "work" is my purpose in life, my discovering of my true self on the journey. Many have taken my places and are doing my "jobs," and in fact, they are doing them better! Nobody can complete my "work" on this earth. Nobody can complete "your work."

That fashioned life of yours, through the work of you and your God, becomes your ultimate yes. Presence, prayer, and participation in your every NOW belong only to you and can only be given away by you.

It is critical to remain cognizant of our immense gifts and understand God's loving expectations. This is why we pause, pray and humbly utter our yes.

"Prayer is sitting in the silence until it silences us, choosing gratitude until we are grateful and praising God until we ourselves are an act of praise." Richard Rohr, OFM

Action Step: (Spiritual Plane)

In summary, then, course corrections unfold my daily awareness:

The physical plane is seen as my own journey here on earth, NOW.

The mental plane is known as my faced truth in every NOW.

The spiritual plane is resourced and honored as my unconditional power source, NOW!

Yes!

Many are praying for the holy woman who established the Sisters of the Incarnate Word communities of women, in France, to be raised from Venerable to being recognized in the Church as Saint. Venerable Jeanne Chézard de Matel's words were used in the song "Oh, My Gentle Love" and this song can show us how to pray. Her words to Jesus are practical and personal, as our words should also be. Pray for her canonization!

Oh, My Gentle Love

Oh, my Gen-tle Love, choose me as Your friend. Oh, my Gen-tle Love, choose me as Your friend.

1. I sleep in Your arms, In - car - nate Word,_____ lost to my-

self and to all my needs._____ In You are all my hopes and You, Your-

self, are my on - ly con - fi - dence_____ and my e - ter - nal pos - ses - sion.

2. My spir - it is be - fore Your ve - ry eyes._____ My trea-sure is in Your

heart. I want to learn from You._____ What do You want me to do?_____ Speak, Lord, for Your

ser-vant is still, to list - en to You, in peace and tran - quil - i - ty.

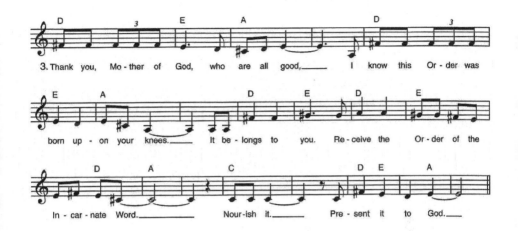

3. Thank you, Mo - ther of God, who are all good,_____ I know this Or - der was

born up - on your knees._____ It be - longs to you. Re - ceive the Or - der of the

In - car - nate Word._____ Nour-ish it._____ Pre - sent it to God._____

October 21, 2003 Music by Patricia Jean Smithyman-Zito   Words adapted from the Writings of Venerable Jeanne Chezard de Matel
www.LivingInTheNowBook.com/music

Course corrections #4 target problem solving and skill mastery on purpose!

Lisa is one of the best Massage Therapists on the West Side of Cleveland. She has established a thriving business and has helped change the daily **NOW** of many grateful people with her intuitive touch and powerful Massage and Thai Massage Therapies. Being her own boss and building a solid business has not been an easy journey. She had to master a variety of skills to live independently in her own home around the age of 25, while building her reputation in the field of massage body work.

There were days when she had no work on the schedule and there were days when the office would have 5 or 6 straight hours of massages on the books. Lisa quickly realized that planning and scheduling would have a positive or negative effect on her business and on her own health! She came to understand the importance of balance in the work world and discipline in her personal wellness.

So she became a skilled Yoga instructor. Yoga practice afforded her scheduled time to repair and build her body, challenged others to become healthy and agile, and blessed her mother with solid and demanding routines that complimented and balanced running! Design your roadmap to wholeness from the inside out and creatively construct your **NOW**, your life!

Course corrections #4 to assure consistent success in your NOW:

A great evening routine not only relaxes you, but also recharges you for the next day so you can show up in an optimum physical, mental and emotional state. Here are five effective evening habits to set yourself up for success the following day:

1. Identify your three biggest tasks for tomorrow.

The possibility of getting sidetracked from living fully in your NOW is more likely to happen when you don't have a plan you can follow consistently. Without taking a moment to think about what's essential, you run the risk of being busy instead of being productive, efficient and effective in your NOW.

Identifying your three biggest tasks for the next day allows you to head into the day with clarity, direction and purpose. To determine your biggest goals ask yourself, *If I don't get anything else done tomorrow, what are the three biggest and most effective tasks that can keep me centered in my NOW?*

I set daily reminder alarms on my Google Calendar for just about everything and it frees up my mind while it keeps me on task. It is free, too!

2. Move your body.

Pretend your health is the head of an octopus. Without that head operating efficiently, those tentacles aren't going to perform to their capabilities. After a hard day at work, exercising removes the clutter in your head, relieves stressors, and thus creates space for new ideas, positive thoughts and a deep appreciation of your NOW.

Whether it's a quick 30-minute gym workout, a mile-run in the park, a relaxing yoga class or even a social activity such as salsa dancing, any type of movement will allow you to experience the positive endorphins that exercise provides.

3. Make time for those closest to you.

One of the best ways to maintain your happiness and recharge after a long day is to dedicate time to your relationships. Relationships are a powerful driving force behind our happiness and it's those people who are our biggest supporters during good and bad times. Make it a nightly goal to give your uninterrupted attention to those closest to you. The activity doesn't matter so much as just spending mutual NOW time together.

4. Educate yourself.

To become the most successful version of yourself, build a mindset of continuous learning. You're not only increasing your intelligence, but you're also fueling yourself with valuable inspiration. Inspirational fuel boosts positive thoughts as you sleep and helps you wake up with an optimistic state of mind. Commit to a nightly reading goal of 30 minutes.

5. Give gratitude and reflect on the day.

As we work toward our goals, it's easy to get lost in the chase and forget to acknowledge what we already have. Instituting a nightly gratitude habit keeps you grounded in the present moment while allowing you to stay motivated. End your day by writing three to four positive things that happened that day. A grateful heart is a happy heart.

_____

_____

_____

_____

_____

_____

_____

_____

_____

_____

I pray that we may always be present to holiness, to purpose, to this incarnational birthing and fleshing of eternal love. We really must taste and see, reflecting and responding constantly! Only then can we, through the "almostness" of living life to the fullest, even begin our "job" here on this earth. Our "work" is forever expressed in the core truth of our very existence. We now can identify with our soul, not our ego!

You are God's unending truth! Glorifying God in you proclaims your soul's work on earth and your personal conquering of the physical and mental planes for all eternity! One last song petitions Mary, the mother of Jesus, to teach us how to love!

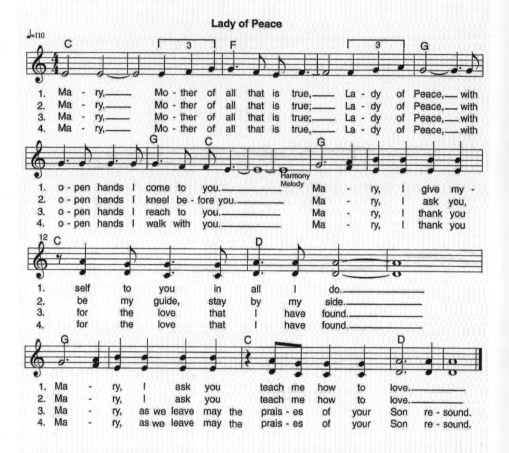

Lady of Peace

♩=110

1. Ma - ry,_____ Mo - ther of all that is true,_____ La - dy of Peace,_____ with
2. Ma - ry,_____ Mo - ther of all that is true;_____ La - dy of Peace,_____ with
3. Ma - ry,_____ Mo - ther of all that is true;_____ La - dy of Peace,_____ with
4. Ma - ry,_____ Mo - ther of all that is true,_____ La - dy of Peace,_____ with

1. o - pen hands I come to you._____ Ma - ry, I give my -
2. o - pen hands I kneel be - fore you._____ Ma - ry, I ask you,
3. o - pen hands I reach to you._____ Ma - ry, I thank you
4. o - pen hands I walk with you._____ Ma - ry, I thank you

1. self to you in all I do._____
2. be my guide, stay by my side._____
3. for the love that I have found._____
4. for the love that I have found._____

1. Ma - ry, I ask you teach me how to love._____
2. Ma - ry, I ask you teach me how to love._____
3. Ma - ry, as we leave may the prais - es of your Son re - sound.
4. Ma - ry, as we leave may the prais - es of your Son re - sound.

Read after verse 1:
Yes, how I long to love in the gentlest of ways.
And, as a new beginning in my life becomes a reality,
I kneel before you and I pray...

Read after verse 2:
Family, my hopes and dreams of the future
will grow from the seeds of love planted here.
And as our love begins to blossom
here at your Son's altar, I pray...

Read after verse 3:
Peace, we can experience ever so much peace
if our lives revolve around those we love.
And as we love others, we spread your Son's peace,
and live as you have taught us. So now I pray...

Note: *While reading, guitarist picks
the chords G, C, D, G, C, D...*

May 8, 1976 Words and Music by Patricia Jean Smithyman-Zito.

www.LivingInTheNowBook.com/music

May we all live each day in an attitude of contemplation and praise, with a heart's desire to be the face of God in our world, NOW.

Action Step: (Join our Living in the NOW community!)
www.LivingInTheNowBook.com/journey

This book is a checklist, a to-do list, a short-cut and a new beginning for making each day your best, NOW. It is humbly presented by someone who has learned expansion along the way. Congratulations on completing our journal work together.

The journey to Living in the NOW is an ongoing process and I would love to help support you along the way. Join our Living in the NOW community, where we share many more course corrections, resources, stories, songs and prayer experiences. You know the link! www.LivingInTheNowBook.com/journey

The internet will have to unite us for now. In heaven, we will all be living on the same street!

"Begin doing what you want to do NOW. We are not living in eternity. We have only this moment, sparkling like a star in our hand and melting like a snowflake. Let us use it before it is too late."
Marie Beyon Ray

"Praised be the Incarnate Word, now and forever. Amen."
Venerable Jeanne Chézard de Matel, Foundress of the Sisters of the Incarnate Word Religious Communities around the world.

May you live fully in the NOW, being worthy of this journey you are given to bring God's Word to life by unconditional love.

God's best, my prayers and an alleluia for 40 days of journey work to live fully in the NOW!

Patricia Jean Smithyman-Zito
pjzito@zitoprohealth.com

Other resources for inspiration and insights you may enjoy are:

www.gratefulness.org - This site can be your online sanctuary that shares the power of being grateful!
www.sacredspace.ie - This is a prayer website that has been around since 1999!
www.cac.org/ - This is the Center for Action and Contemplation and the Richard Rohr Institute - I have been to the Center in Albuquerque, New Mexico several times!
www.LivingInTheNowBook.com/spiritual - Contemporary Christian singers and uplifting songs can be found here, too!

A great book for awareness of LIVING IN THE NOW is Mitch Albom's bestseller "Tuesdays with Morrie: An Old Man, a Young Man, and Life's Greatest Lesson" and it is a memoir that chronicles weekly visits Albom made to see his former sociology professor, Morrie Schwartz. Schwartz is gradually losing his life to ALS and Albom's journal speaks of coming to understand the wisdom and happiness Morrie shows him and how to ensure you are LIVING IN THE NOW! Here is a quote from the book: "As you grow, you learn more. If you stayed as ignorant as you were at twenty-two, you'd always be twenty-two. Aging is not just decay, you know. It's growth. It's more than the negative that you're going to die, it's the positive that you understand you're going to die, and that you live a better life because of it."

My friend for over 50 years, Barb V, just gifted me with an amazing book called "Journeys with the Messiah" - This fashion photographer, Michael Belk, explores the modern-day relevance of Jesus with pictures and commentary! He traded in his glamorous globe-trotting lifestyle to share the life and impact of Jesus through the lens of his camera! Meet Jesus in your NOW with this!

"Success is getting what you want. Happiness is wanting what you get."
Dale Carnegie

Past work:

1. Contributing composer, musician and vocalist, with 23 other members of the Sisters of the Incarnate Word Community in Cleveland, Ohio, to an LP album of original songs released in 1974, titled "Composed for You." My songs from this album: Getting Excited, Speak to Me of Life, I Belong to You, Composed for You and Everybody Knows this Man are used with permission of the copyright holder, Sisters of the Incarnate Word, Parma Heights, Ohio.

2. A nationwide 16mm film was produced, in 1976, by St. Paul Technical Institute for the Deaf of 3 of PJ's original songs performed by her in sign language. Sold through NAD to the deaf and hard of hearing communities, all profits from the film titled "Composed for You" were donated to the school.

3. Voted "Woman of the Year" in 1990.
   Eastlake Woman's Club
   1580 E332nd St.
   Eastlake, OH 44095
   Serving the community since 1965.

4. "Composed for You – Companions on the Journey," a poetry book, was published in 2010. That book includes all of the poems found in this work and is available at www. LivingInTheNowBook.com/poetry

Used for the 40 Days of Lent, young adult leadership groups, spirituality groups, retreat settings, relationship support settings, personal growth, parenting with purpose, health and wellness, grief recovery, varied educational support settings like Confirmation Programs and many more transformational encounters!

This book changes the every day awareness of our surroundings and expands intentional purpose for each day.

Together, we shed our egos and our truth turns into rocket fuel for expanded consciousness, changing our world and inspiring others by the every-day-abundance shared when LIVING IN THE NOW!

"When you have done everything that you can do, surrender. Give yourself up to the power and energy that's greater than yourself."
Oprah Winfrey

"God has given us two hands, one to receive with and the other to give with." Billy Graham

Your NOW contains all you ever need!
Keep those hands open!
PJ Zito